A TALE OF
TWO SISTERS

An original screenplay by

Paul Breeze

Suitable for Film or TV Drama

This screenplay is available for licensing to professional TV or film companies.

In the first instance, please contact the publishers by email at
info@poshupnorth.com

First published in Great Britain in October 2012 by
Posh Up North Publishing
Nightingale Cottage, Reedley Hallows BB9 5JG/3

Original Story © 2003
This Edition © 2012 Paul Breeze

British Library cataloguing in publication data.
A catalogue record for this book is available from the British Library

ISBN: 978-0-9539782-8-1

Interesting Books...
...Fascinating Subjects!

POSH UP NORTH
Publishing
www.poshupnorth.com

List Of Characters

Angela Davison - Former ballet dancer, stuck with violent husband

Norman Davison - Disgraced Army officer, would-be businessman

Darren Davison - The couple's son

Sonya Davison - Daughter

Margaret Gordon - Angela's mother.

Jim - Norman's site manager and Angela's confidante

Barry "Baz" Davison - Norman's brother – a lawyer.

Lucy Gordon - Angela's sister.

Bradford Yorkes - Former ballet dancer pal of Angela's

Karl Sänger - Former love of Angela's

Phil - Private detective

Opening Sequence: *EXT – SPANISH LANDSCAPE - DAY*

The scene is idyllic sun drenched Spanish countryside. It is a hot sunny afternoon. All is quiet and peaceful. In the background we hear soothing Spanish guitar music. The camera slowly pans to settle upon a country house with a large garden and swimming pool next to it.

The sound of a breaking glass breaks the peaceful silence.

Another crash and sounds of cursing. Our view jolts round to look at an open doorway.

Another shout and we look to see a blonde head looking cautiously over the top of a low wall across the other side of the swimming pool.

> NORMAN (unseen)
> You bitch!

A figure comes stumbling out of the doorway.

> NORMAN (slurred speech)
> Where have you put it?

Cut to scene behind the wall. The blonde head ducks down. We see a woman in her late 30s/ early 40s cowering and clutching two children aged 14/ 15 closely to her. A dog also sits shaking and cowering with the group.

Off camera, we hear the sounds of furniture being knocked over and more shouts. The woman winces and cowers with each outburst.

Opening Titles Run:

Black and white footage of a single ballet dancer practising steps and jumps interspersed with black and white footage of 1960s Berlin gradually introducing film of British soldiers having fun at dances etc ending with shaky (handshot) footage of ballet dancer and army officer getting marriedas the couple leave the church, a line of army officers raise their swords and a line of ballet dancers raise their shoes.

Scene 1: EXT – SHOPPING STREET – DAY

A busy shopping street in Gibraltar. Lots of people bustling round. Zoom in on a clothes shop with lots of clothes rails outside.

MARGARET and ANGELA are looking at dresses. There is some discussion. They go into the shop and come out carrying several large bags.

Scene 2: INT – COFFEE SHOP – DAY

MARGARET and ANGELA are having coffee and cakes

> ANGELA
> I still wonder if I shouldn't have taken the blue instead…?
> It would go with those shoes I bought in Spain you know

> MARGARET
> Blue, pink, it's all the same if you never go anywhere in it! When I was your age, daddy and I used to go out at least twice a week…to a restaurant or the theatre…

> ANGELA
> Yes, but you know how hard Norman is working at the moment. Once we get the foundations down for the site, the money will start pouring in and we'll have lots more time together and he won't drink so much. He'll be less stressed.

> MARGARET
> Huh! If you believe that, you'll believe anything. You know as well as I do he'll try anything to avoid doing a good days work. Fancy paying all that money to rent that huge office.

He spends most of his time asleep in there you know. I sometimes wish I'd stayed back in England...

ANGELA
Oh! Don't say that Mummy. You know I only agreed to come here because it seemed the best for everyone. Anyway, **we're** having fun aren't we...?

Waitress comes with bill. ANGELA makes no movement to look at it. MARGARET snorts and picks up the bill and pays it. She counts the money from her purse very carefully.

MARGARET
Seventy.....eighty..... five. Hmm I'm getting a bit short. Luckily my next cheque should be here in a day or two.

ANGELA
Hmm, I think we'll need to talk about that....

Scene 3: INT – Norman's OFFICE - DAY

Big painted sign on wall reads "Davison Developments". The block looks very chic and expensive. The office is furnished with huge luxurious looking leather chairs and a huge desk. A secretary's desk to one side has unopened boxes of computer equipment and new filing cabinets are waiting to be unpacked.

In contrast, the office floor is cluttered with bits of paper, unopened letters (bills) and the bin is full of empty bottles. NORMAN sits laid back in his big directors chair feet on the desk, telephone to his ear.

> NORMAN
> Well, yes, actually, if you check the records, you'll see that I actually resigned as a director of that particular company before the transaction went through.
>
> OK, yes I am still a shareholder but it's a limited company and I only have a 1% share. Would you like that? No, I appreciate it won't help you get your joists back. But, as you can see, there's nothing I can personally do about it... really sorry.

He leans across and knocks on the surface of his desk.

> NORMAN
> Sorry, someone at the door, gotta go. Hope you get sorted out.

He puts phone down. Breaths a sigh of relief and takes a half empty bottle from desk draw, leans back in chair and takes a couple of deep swigs. Picks up phone and dials long distance number.
> NORMAN
> Hi Baz! It's Norm. Yes, not so bad. How's it going with the offer?. We really don't want the old woman to have to get involved with it. She'll ruin everything. Anyway round it? Hmm yes..... could it really work?

A silhouette appears outside the door. A little knock is followed by ANGELA `s smiling face peering round the edge of the door.

*NORMAN gestures that he will free in a minute and she shuts the
door again.*

                    NORMAN
          Ok listen Baz! I've got to go. The old ball and chain's
          here. Yes you sort it all out at your end. I`ll find a way
          to get her to sign it without them knowing what it is.
          Speak soon.

He puts the phone down and calls ANGELA in.

                    NORMAN
          Right darling - all finished for today. Big deal going
          through. Should make us a packet. But don't you
          worry your pretty little head about that. Let's go and
          have something to eat eh...? Has your mum's
          cheque got here yet...?

Scene 4: INT – KITCHEN – EVENING

The family are sitting around a big table in a rustic looking kitchen. Pots and plates are piled up to show that a good meal is nearing its close. There are three empty wine bottles in front of NORMAN, who looks rather dishevelled. A heavy discussion is ensuing. NORMAN seems to be interrogating everyone about something very minor.

NORMAN
But the post office said that a letter came today from England. Did it or didn't it?

ANGELA
Well Mum and I were in town shopping most of the day as you know so I wouldn't have seen it anyway.

NORMAN
Yes and you came to the office suite for me from at 5, where did mum go then?

ANGELA
Oh, she got a taxi home said she was tired.

MARGARET
I certainly was. She spent all afternoon trying to decide on the blue dress in Marples or the pink one at the other end of town.. The heat's not good for me here. I wish I was back in London.

NORMAN turns on MARGARET and announces in triumph

NORMAN
So you were here on your own when you get back from town! I thought as much. Was there a letter here or not?

MARGARET
Can't say as I remember seeing a letter. Certainly not one for you anyway, even if there was one. Not that I'm saying there was.

NORMAN stands up aggressively and turns on MARGARET

> NORMAN
> Don't start your dotty old woman act again! You always put it on to annoy me! Did your bloody cheque turn up or not?

ANGELA tries to intervene

> ANGELA
> Oh Norman, don't start a fight please not tonight. I thought you'd had a good day at the office. You said you had. I was hoping things would be nice tonight that's why I cooked such a nice dinner.

NORMAN turns towards his wife, hand half raised as if to hit her. He then takes a deep breath and sits down again in a sulk. Everyone sighs a sigh of relief and continues eating their dessert, not daring to look up. After a few seconds of deathly silence, a small voice chirps up:

> SONYA
> Daddy, there's a field trip for school next week and I need the money by Friday. You did say I could go.

> DARREN
> Oh yeah, dad, I need some more football boots as well, otherwise I can't play on Saturday.

NORMAN is torn between flying at the kids and wanting to show a fatherly benignness. In the end he mumbles:

> NORMAN
> You know you should ask mum for things like that. I don't carry much cash around. It's all tied up in the business.

> MARGARET
> Business hah! What business? Monkey business more like! When are we going to see this

development of yours? It's just a bit of old wasteland not a thing done on it in 6 months…

NORMAN
I told you she's not senile! Doesn't miss a thing. You ought to keep your nose out of things you don't understand!

NORMAN goes to open his 4th bottle of wine, spilling some of it as he pours into his glass.

MARGARET
I may be old but I do know that drinking solves nothing! Pull yourself together!

Before NORMAN can react, ANGELA leaps up and starts clearing away the dishes

ANGELA
Right kids, bedtime I think

DARREN
Aw mum, what about….

ANGELA
Bed now!

She motions towards NORMAN who is still knocking back the wine. The kids understand that a withdrawal might be in order.

DARREN and SONYA get up from the table, kiss MARGARET and ANGELA and go to bed. MARGARET also takes her chance to escape the inquisition.

MARGARET
Yes, I think I`ll go up now too.   Church in the morning you know…

NORMAN stands up and shouts up the stairs after her.

NORMAN
It's not bloody Sunday tomorrow you silly woman!
You haven't been to church for ages anyway.

He rounds on ANGELA and continues his tirade:

NORMAN
She's bloody well putting that on. I know her cheque
arrived today and I want it! You'll have to get it off
her tomorrow.

ANGELA
But Norman, it is her money after all.

NORMAN
Yes and we're looking after her, that costs a bloody
fortune! It'd be cheaper to put her in a home!

ANGELA
But then you wouldn't get you hands on her money,
would you..?

*NORMAN slaps ANGELA hard across the face in anger. She falls
back into her chair in a flood of tears. He first goes to console her but
instead grabs his bottle and storms out of the kitchen in the direction
of the living room, stumbles over the dog as he goes and
unnecessarily kicks her in admonition.*

Scene 5: INT – KITCHEN - NIGHT

NORMAN arrives home late. He slumps down in the dark and empty kitchen. There is just a small candle in the middle of the table. He takes some pieces of paper from his jacket pocket. They are gambling IOUs he holds each one over the candle flame and burns them.

NORMAN stands up and looks in the fridge. ANGELA has left him a cold meat salad covered in clingfilm with a little note: "Missed you at tea time, love Angie xxxx" He takes the plate and throws it against the wall. The dog comes to see what is going on and is quickly sent away on the end of his foot with a sorry yelp.

NORMAN storms upstairs and drags ANGELA out of bed, screaming at her and hitting her

> NORMAN
> You lazy bitch! I've been out all day long working hard for all of us and all you can be bothered to do is leave me a note in the fridge with a poxy lettuce leaf!
>
> Get down there and cook me something decent now!

ANGELA is still trying to wake up properly as her shakes her and hits her around the head and body.

At that moment, the bedroom door is thrown open and the light switched on. MARGARET is standing there with a heavy poker in her hand. For once she is perfectly sentient and normal. She commands NORMAN:

> MARGARET
> Leave her alone you brute! If I ever see you lay a finger on her again, I will call the police!

Stunned by this intrusion, NORMAN throws ANGELA back onto the bed and storms out of the bedroom. MARGARET stays to comfort ANGELA

Scene 6: INT – AIRPORT - DAY

NORMAN is standing in the arrivals area looking out for someone coming through the arrivals gate. He is casually dressed in cool-looking clothes as is everyone else in the vicinity.

He suddenly catches sight of his brother walking through the arrivals gate and waves at him. Baz looks very hot and out of place. He is wearing a heavy blue suit and tie, carrying a heavy overcoat and a briefcase.

> NORMAN
> I got your message – why all the rush?.....

> BAZ
> God, it's bloody hot here isn't it – it's chucking it down at home.
> Thought I'd better get this stuff to you as soon as possible – didn't want it hanging around the office..

> NORMAN
> Well, yeah – understandable I suppose - so you've got it with you..?

> BAZ
> Come on, I don't want to talk here – is your car nearby...?

> NORMAN
> Just outside, come on – where's your luggage?

The pair walk out of the airport and cross the road to where Norman's car is parked in the short stay bays. They drive off.

Scene 7: IN CAR – DAY

Norman is driving through Spanish looking streets.

BAZ
So, did you get away without your little ballet dancer
knowing where you were going?

NORMAN
Yeah – just told her I had some business – I'm boss
in my own house, you know..

BAZ
That's good, don't forget you said I could have a go
with her when I sorted this all out for you

NORMAN
Yeah, yeah sure – so you've actually got it with you?

BAZ
Certainly have – all you've got to do to is get the old
bag and the girl to sign it and it's all yours.

NORMAN
So how did you manage it? I asked around and the
local briefs said that the old witch had to be
interviewed in person and be certified loopy by two
independent professionals.

BAZ
Very good question – and normally very hard to get
round but, on this occasion we had a little bit of luck.

One of our solicitors is retiring on health grounds –
bit of a sob story really but, if he can't hack it, he's no
use to have around.

Anyway, I have to sign his release so that he can get
his pension.

I hauled him in and basically told him that if he didn't sign the certification, I'd refer his case on and that would hold it up for months so, he signed the power of attourney and I seconded it.

What was hers is now ANGELA's and what's ANGELA's is, of course,yours…

Baz smiles at Norman. Norman grins back. The car drives on towards the town centre.

Scene 8: INT – OFFICE - DAY

Norman and BAZ enter Norman's office. Baz takes the papers out of his case and Norman locks them in one of his desk drawers. He pulls out a bottle of scotch and two glasses and they toast their success.

The scene fades and returns a couple of hours later. The pair are still drinking and are obviously becoming drunk.

> NORMAN
> You're sure you can't stop for a few days? There's plenty of room…

> BAZ
> No, I'm booked on tonight's flight back – don't want to draw too much attention to our little deal eh…

The telephone on the desk rings. Norman picks it up – it is ANGELA on the other end of the line.

> NORMAN
> Yes darling, I'm back – no, nothing important.
> Hmm, yes, OK well. See you later then.

He puts the phone down and asides to BAZ

> NORMAN
> That was the old trouble and strife – checking up on me.

NORMAN begins to giggle drunkenly

> NORMAN
> She… she thinks it's so that she can get medical fees paid for her old ma, the daft cow! Not that she's bothered so long as she can go out and buy her pretty dresses and her twee little make up.

> BAZ
> That reminds me – you need to pay up on our deal.

NORMAN
Eh,... what do you mean...?

BAZ
You said that if I got the paper work done so that you
had control over Margie's businesses, then I could
shag your ANGELA

NORMAN
Well, yeah but I didn't think you really meant it – we
were pissed at the time... did I really..?

BAZ
Yes, you bloody did. And if you don't cough up, I'll
take the papers back and you'll have to wait for the
old witch to die and that'll take years...

The office door swings open and ANGELA pops her head in.

ANGELA
Hello darling! I finished early so I thought I'd come
and surprise you – oh...!

She sees Baz slumped back in a chair grinning.

ANGELA
Barry! I didn't know you were coming . Norman why
didn't you tell me? I've got nothing ready at the
house...

*BAZ jumps up and goes over to her, putting his arm round her
shoulders.*

BAZ
No need love – just a flying visit with some papers
for Norm to sign – I'm on my way soon. How are
you? You are looking lovely.

*BAZ leads her over to the sofa and sits her down next to him. He
turns to Norman and whispers:*

Time to pay up – give us some privacy eh..?

BAZ motions his head towards the door. Norman looks upset and starts to protest

                    NORMAN
          Come on, Baz, she's my wife…

BAZ makes a sterner motion towards the door with gritted teeth. ANGELA watches the scene open mouthed, not sure what is going on. NORMAN goes to leave the room, his head dropped.

                    ANGELA
          Norman – what's going on.. Barry.. don't!…

NORMAN leaves the room and slowly pulls the door behind him. Over his should we see BAZ putting his hand on ANGELA'S knee and slowly moving it up her thigh. She tries to pull away but he holds her closely to him.

Outside the office door, NORMAN leans back against the wall, looking up at the ceiling. He slowly exhales. From inside we hear ANGELA calling him to come back. NORMAN slowly walks away down the corridor.

Scene 9: INT – LOBBY – DAY

NORMAN is sitting in the reception area on the ground floor of the office block, nervously reading the paper and constantly looking to the lift.

The lift bell rings, the door opens and BAZ comes out looking hot and bothered, trying to tuck his shirt into his trousers whilst carrying his jacket coat and case at the same time.

NORMAN just stands there staring, not sure what to say. BAZ blusters past him..

> BAZ
> Well, that was a bloody disappointment – waited years for that and she wails all the way through – some wife you've got…

NORMAN goes to remonstrate with his brother but is waved away.

> BAZ
> No need to drive me to the airport, I'll get a taxi. Just remember, if any of this comes back at me you're in it too…

NORMAN stands open mouthed as BAZ storms out of the building and flags down a passing taxi. BAZ disappears leaving NORMAN on his own in the lobby.

After a few moments, NORMAN goes to the lift and goes in it.

We cut to see him sheepishly entering his office where ANGELA is sitting on the floor crying, her eyes are red and blotchy and she is rearranging her clothes, some of which look torn.

She looks up at NORMAN and then turns her head away in disgust.

FADE

Scene 10: INT – APARTMENT BEDROOM - DAY

Room is small and untidy as if a bachelor pad. There is a huge bed in the middle of the room. A TV and hi-fi system are in easy reach and an ensuite bathroom to one side. ANGELA is tucked up in bed, her clothes folded neatly on a nearby chair.

A young man emerges from the shower with just a towel around him. He lets the towel drop and slides into bed beside ANGELA she smiles and snuggles up to him.

> ANGELA
> God Jim, I don't know what I'd do if it wasn't for you. I think I'd go crazy.

Jim mumbles some sort of agreement as if he isn't really listening. He is too busy kissing her neck and shoulder.

> ANGELA
> And none of its my fault. I was just doing it for everyone's best interests. Why is it **me** that always comes off worst?

Jim removes himself from ANGELA `s neck and ponders

> JIM
> Sounds to me as if your mum's coming out worst. Sending here to that home like that full of old dodderers. She didn't seem that bad to me.

> ANGELA
> Well, she wasn't really. She put on an act when she didn't want to do something that Norman was making her do. I was worried he might get violent with her. It's better this way really.

> JIM
> And what about her other daughter, the one in Switzerland? Does she know you took power of attorney over all the stuff of your mums?

ANGELA
Lucy? Oh no, we haven't spoken for a while. Anyway
she's got a nicely paid job so she's ok. I'm just
wondering what I should do next.

*The telephone suddenly rings. After a quick stolen kiss, JIM picks it
up.*

JIM
Yes boss, I'm on it right away....

He rolls his eyeballs heavenwards in mock derision of the caller.

JIM
What now Norm? Christ I'm in the middle of
summat... OK... ten minutes.

JIM slams the phone down and starts to get dressed.

JIM
Gotta go honey, your Hubby wants me down on the
building site like yesterday.

*JIM gives ANGELA a quick kiss as he rushes out the door. She
slumps back against the pillow and sighs deeply as if wondering
what to do next.*

Scene 11: INT – APARTMENT BEDROOM - DAY

Bed is unkempt and clothes are scattered around the room. JIM is standing on balcony looking out across the city. ANGELA is sitting in front of the dressing table in a loose dressing gown, humming happily to herself and playing with her hair in the mirror.

> JIM
> I still don't see why…

> ANGELA
> Look Jimmy-hornsters, I told you. I used to say I was visiting Mummy. Now she's gone back to England, Norm'll never let me out. It's only cuz he hated visiting Mummy in that place that he let me out of his sight at all

> JIM
> It wasn't the place he hated, he just couldn't be arsed to pretend to be nice to Marge anymore now he's got his mitts on her money.

> ANGELA
> Oh, don't say it like that. It sounds so callous.

JIM comes in from balcony and stands behind ANGELA he runs his hands over her shoulders and down the front of her dressing gown. She gasps quietly and rubs back against him.

> ANGELA (cont'd)
> Anyway, you know we need the money to bale out the investments. Mmm, don't stop … Anyway, Mummy's being well looked after – better than we could do it. She sent me a postcard the other day saying the new place is fine….mmm

> JIM
> Don't go back, you could stay here with me. You know damn well Norms a bloody wash out.

ANGELA pushes him away and makes as if she wants to leave.

ANGELA
You know I can't leave the kids in this mess and
they'll never leave their dad, I tried, remember back
in England that time….

*JIM stands back but as ANGELA begins to sob he takes her in his
arms to comfort her..*

ANGELA
I'm trapped, I'm bloody stuck. Why? It was such a
good idea! God I miss my mum. Why did daddy have
to die, everything was all right before then….

JIM
Look I'm going to call your sister. Perhaps she can
help. You said she helped before - right? If she's got
as much money as you say, perhaps she could send
you some and you, me and the kids could all get
away from here…leave Norm to his own devices..
what do you say?

Scene 12: INT – LUXURY APARTMENT - NIGHT

dark living room in big luxury flat obviously in a town in central Europe Telephone is ringing on desk. Dark haired lady in mid 40s wearing dressing gown answers telephone.

Scene cuts to Spanish street in semi darkness with lots of neon lights and music in the background. Jim is looking rather dishevelled and glances nervously around as he telephones

> JIM
> Hello.. hello is that Mrs Gordon?... Lucy Gordon?

Scene alternates between Spanish street and Lucy`s apartment.

> LUCY
> Who is that? I can hardly hear you?

> JIM (*trying to shout over music in background*)
> Listen you don't know me but….

> LUCY
> Well, if I don't know you what are you ringing for. Where did you get my number…?

> JIM
> Listen, my name's Jim, I'm a…er friend of Angela's, your sister…?

> LUCY
> Angela..? Where is she? I haven't heard from her for ages… who the hell are you anyway? What's happened?

> JIM
> Well, she's er ok but she needs your help. You've got money yeah? She needs some … They bought a load of old flats over here and it's all gone arse upwards. I've been trying to help but now we've gotta get out… it's turning nasty

LUCY
Flats? What are you talking about? I can hardly hear
you.
Listen **IF** you really do know my sister, then you can
tell her she can bloody well ring me herself. She
knows the number!

LUCY slams the phone down

*JIM hammers on the phone in his phone box but the connection is
broken he searches in his pocket for more change but has none. He
sinks in resignation and leaves the phone box, heading to the
nearest café, looking around paranoically as he goes.*

*LUCY ponders the conversation then leaves the room; the light goes
off, leaving the room dark.*

Scene 13: EXT – SPANISH STREET – NIGHT

The fiesta has finished and the streets are quite. JIM is walking along in a drunken state. He is still looking over his shoulder as if he is being followed. He fumbles a bunch of keys from his pocket and goes towards the entrance door of a block of flats. As he enters the main door, a shadowy figure surprises him.

                    NORMAN (menacingly)
          Hallo Jimbo….! How's it going? Heavy night out?

                    JIM
          God, Norm, you gave me a start. You alright? You
          seem a look a bit pissed to me..

                    NORMAN
          Pissed off more like. Them bastards have done us.
          Foreclosed on the site.

                    JIM
          You're joking. I thought they'd give us another
          extension You said they would. Look do you wanna
          come in? we can see what we can sort out.

                    NORMAN
          No – you come with me. To the site. There's some
          stuff we gotta shift out before they take it over
          tomorrow.

                    JIM
          What…now? It's the almost 4am and you can't
          drive…..

NORMAN grabs JIM roughly and drags him towards a car parked across the street.

                    JIM
          Bloody hell Norm, go careful, OK I'm coming…

They both get into the car. The car lurches off without any lights on.

SCENE 14: INT– BUILDING SITE - NIGHT

NORMAN is sitting at a desk in a caravan going through papers under torchlight. Jim is looking uneasily out of the window.

> **NORMAN**
> I`ll never get through all this lot! Can't tell in this light what's what. We'll have to take the whole caravan and dump the dodgy papers later.

> **JIM**
> Look, I don't know what's going on but I've had enough of this. I was only supposed to be helping you with the building work, nothing crooked, you knew that!

> **NORMAN**
> Surprised you had much time for building.....

> **JIM**
> What do you mean by that?

NORMAN stands up holding his torch menacingly

> **NORMAN**
> You know damn well what I mean. You stitched me up.

> **JIM**
> Hey, calm down mate....

> **NORMAN**
> While you were meant to be out there keeping the blokes on schedule, you were up in your company bloody flat screwing my wife, you bastard!

> **JIM**
> No, Norm, it's not true, honest. She was upset.. all Angela wanted was someone who'd listen to her. Someone to....

                    NORMAN
                    someone to give her a good fucking because I didn't
                    fancy her anymore .. is that it?

*NORMAN swaggers towards Jim looking all the more agitated and
aggressive*

                    NORMAN (*continued*)
                    Well ,that's all wrong. She was completely fucking
                    useless! Didn't have a single idea in her stupid head.

NORMAN bangs his hand on the desk. Jim cowers away.

                    NORMAN (*continued*)
                    She didn't even have the fucking inheritance she
                    made me think she'd got- all went to her poncey
                    bloody sister didn't it.....

                    JIM
                    Hey, Norm, I don't know nothing about that, all I was
                    doing....

                    NORMAN
                    Laughing at me! - the pair of you, behind my back...
                    well no more!

*JIM tries to back away but comes up against the filing cabinet
NORMAN swings at JIM with his torch. Jim trips and bangs his head
against the corner of the table as he falls.*

                    NORMAN
                    No more ... do you hear...?!

*NORMAN drops to his knees next to JIM`s body and proceeds to hit
it mercilessly with the end of the torch until NORMAN collapses
across the body in gasps and floods of tears.*

Scene 15: EXT – HACIENDA – DAY

The Volvo and caravan are parked outside the house. The family are frantically rushing back and forth loading things into both and getting in each others way.

> NORMAN
> Hurry up for god's sake! we should have been left ages ago!

> SONYA
> But daddy why must we leave now…I've got my horse riding lesson tonight and school tomorrow – couldn't we wait until the end of term?

NORMAN drops what he's carrying and grabs SONYA by the shoulders, shouting into her face.

> NORMAN
> You do as you're bloody well told and don't argue!

> NORMAN (*more calmly*)
> Look honey, I'm sorry. Things have just got a little on top of me. There are some people coming to buy the house and I don't want to be here when they arrive,, OK? We're just going on a little holiday.

> DARREN
> But dad, who's going to let them into to look round…..

> NORMAN
> Don't worry about that… they'll let themselves in, let's just hurry up eh?

ANGELA comes out of house with a huge pile of hat boxes and handbags..

> ANGELA
> Right, I've managed to narrow it down to these but if it turns cold, I`ll need to get my boots as well.

NORMAN
Which bag has got the passports and papers in?

ANGELA
This one here

NORMAN
Right dump the rest of that crap and let's go

NORMAN takes the rest of the hats and bags and throws them to one side, pushing ANGELA towards the car. DARREN lets the dog into the caravan and closes the door. The children both get into the back of the car.

Norman is at the wheel, the car speeds off up the country lane with the caravan swinging behind it.

Scene 16: INT – LIVING ROOM – DAY

We are in the front room of a small and shabby looking terraced house in Bradford. The family's belongings are laying around in boxes waiting to be unpacked. DARREN and SONYA are lounging around watching television, completely oblivious to the mess. ANGELA is trying to lay the table for lunch, walking around piles of boxes and tripping over things on the floor as she brings things in from the kitchen.

        ANGELA
        Come on then, dinner's on the table

        DARREN
        Oh mum, we're watching this….

        ANGELA
        I don't care… at least we'll do this right even if everything else is such an awful bloody mess, now come to the table …

        DARREN
        But dad's not here yet.

        ANGELA
        Just do as you're told!

Door opens and NORMAN walks in looking quite pleased with himself. He is carrying lots of envelopes and booklets. The kids quickly jump up from the settee and obediently sit at the table.

        ANGELA
        How did you get on darling? Find anything..?

        NORMAN
        Yes lots of things…it's looking pretty good

NORMAN starts flicking through his papers and laying them out across the table around the dinner plates.

ANGELA
Oh, I knew you'd have no trouble getting a job with all your training and experience..!

NORMAN
Job? You must be joking. This stuff's much better. Now let me see.... there's housing benefit... council rebates..... kids at school... yes that's two lots of child benefit....

ANGELA
I THOUGHT you were going to the job centre to find a job...

NORMAN
Well, I was but then I passed the benefits agency and saw all this lot.
I reckon that with my army pension and your mum's money and this little lot we'll be well away and won't have to work again..!

DARREN
What, like be on holiday the whole time? Sounds cool....

ANGELA
But you can't just not work, Norman, its...

NORMAN
It's....? It's what? I'll tell you what it is. Bloody pointless! I got blown up for my country in Cyprus and then blown out in Spain. That's where work gets you. Not me, no more, I've had it. They've screwed me enough and now I'm going to screw them.

ANGELA
But we can't use Mummy's money, Not now she's not living with us. That's not fair on her.

NORMAN
Not fair on her? What about us? We had to put up
with her all that time, drag her halfway across
Europe with us..... she was off her head half the time
and incontinent the rest! Don't you think we deserve
something out of it?

Anyway, if it wasn't for us she wouldn't be in that
nice home...and that costs a bloody fortune...

ANGELA
Well, I suppose it is the best place for her, isn't is.
We wouldn't have room for her here now anyway.
Maybe we ought to go and see her now we're
back...

*NORMAN grunts and starts tucking into this food. The others follow
suit. ANGELA sighs to herself and looks rather disappointed at how
things are going.*

Scene 17: EXT – RESIDENTIAL HOME – DAY

It's a bleak, grey and windy scene. The Byron Dobson Home For Retired Folk looks a very remote and forbidding place. Set in it's own grounds with a long drive leading up to it from the village road.

Scene 18: INT – MARGARET`s ROOM – DAY

Margaret is furiously fumbling through a draw containing papers. She looks up at the clock, then to the window, then continues with her task. She takes what looks like building society books and cheque books, and leaves the room, glancing up at the clock again..

She goes to another room along the corridor, knocks on the door and goes in.

> MARGARET
> Cooee, Hilda it's only me, Margie..

> HILDA
> Hello Margie, cup of tea..?

> MARGARET
> No time at the moment I'm afraid. My daughter's coming to see me.

> HILDA
> Oh, that'll be nice.....

> MARGARET
> Well, it would be.. except that no good husband'll be coming with her...

> HILDA
> Ooh yes.. you told me about him didn't you.....nasty piece of work - Nigel, Nathan ... or something...

MARGARET
Norman, actually – curse the man. I don't know what
she sees in him. Knocks her about you know... I've
seen it.

HILDA (eyes widening in fear)
Oh dear and now he's coming here...

MARGARET
Yes he's after money, you can be sure of that. Here,
look after these for me till he `s gone, will you....

HILDA
Of course, love. What is it.

MARGARET
Oh, it's my bank books and papers. He'll go fiddling
through my drawers if he gets the chance. I don't
want him to see them...

MARGARET looks up at the clock and makes for the door.

MARGARET
I`d better get back. I've got more things to hide
before they get here....See you later.

*MARGARET goes back to her room and frantically starts trying to
hide the silver photo frames that she has on the sideboard, looking
anxiously at the clock and out of the window. Through the window
we see the Volvo slowly approaching up the drive.*

Scene 19: INT – ENTRANCE HALL – DAY

NORMAN and ANGELA enter the home. NORMAN makes directly for the stairs.

> NORMAN
> Why don't you go and see the matron, make sure everything's in order. I`ll go and find mum's room..

The scene alternates between MARGARET in her room trying to find a hiding place for one last piece of silver and NORMAN going along the corridor looking at each room number to find the right one.

Finally NORMAN arrives at the right door. His hand touches the handle. MARGARET senses this and sits down in her armchair, stuffing the ornament down the side as the door opens.

> NORMAN
> Hello Mum! How are you? I've so much been looking forward to seeing you after so long…

> MARGARET
> It's not time for my tablets yet doctor… it's only three o'clock…

> NORMAN
> No mum, I'm not the doctor, it's me…Norman, Angela's husband…

> MARGARET
> Norman… no, no, no. the doctor's not called Norman, he's called Arthur. Doctor Arthur. You must have the wrong patient. Doctor.

> NORMAN (*dropping his act*)
> Don't start that play acting with me again. You know bloody well I'm your son in law, Norman Davison – Angela's husband.

MARGARET
No, haven't got a son. Daughter yes, Now, what's
her name...

NORMAN looks about to explode when there is a tap at the door.
ANGELA rushes in and gives her mum a hug.

ANGELA
Oh, hello Mummy! How are you feeling? The matron
says you've been feeling better again now...

MARGARET (dropping her act just a little)
Angie – what a lovely surprise... have you come
straight from school? is Lucy with you?.

ANGELA
No Mummy, Lucy`s in Switzerland working, you
know that. Norman brought me here. Didn't you
darling....

NORMAN (back to the act)
That's right. All the way from Bradford. We're living in
Bradford now you know. Not too far way so we can
come and see you much more often....

MARGARET (under her breath)
Heaven forbid!

ANGELA , sensing the icy atmosphere tries to break the ice by
thrusting a bunch of flowers under MARGARET `s nose.

ANGELA
Look Mummy. We've brought you some flowers. I`ll
go and get some water.

MARGARET goes to get up but ANGELA has already gone.
Sensing his chance, NORMAN starts looking through the drawers.

MARGARET
What are you doing, doctor??

NORMAN (*searching through drawers and looking at papers*)
Cut the act, I need the deeds for the London properties…they need, erm, updating,

MARGARET leaps to her feet and faces up to him

MARGARET
Updating my foot! You want to steal them, you and that crooked brother of yours. You've already stolen my home and now you want my rents as well. Well, I won't have it. I'm going to stop you.

NORMAN pushes MARGARET back into her chair. She is about to get up again when ANGELA comes back, accompanied by HILDA.

ANGELA
Look mummy, this nice lady has made some tea for us all.

HILDA (with a knowing nod)
Thought you might be ready for one, dear

The four sit down to have tea in an uneasy silence. ANGELA tries to engage HILDA in small talk whilst MARGARET and NORMAN glare at each other across the room.

Scene 20: INT – NORMAN & ANGELAS BEDROOM – DAY

We fade to look at the bedside clock. It says 10. 00am. Laying on the bedside table next to the clock are some opened envelopes and a couple of cheques – one for £4.000 made out to Mrs Angela Davison, POA Margaret Gordon.

In the background we hear a creaking bed and gasps ands sighs.

We move our view outwards and see NORMAN and ANGELA making love on the bed. It is a very enthusiastic looking love scene with ANGELA obviously a willing partner, clinging onto the headboard.

She gasps with pleasure and NORMAN grunts with a final effort, then he rolls over and lays flat, breathing heavily.

> NORMAN
> Ooh, that felt good!

> ANGELA
> Phew, you're telling me. How long has it been? And during the day as well, it feels ever so naughty..!

> NORMAN
> Yes, this is the life, no more working for me.

NORMAN rolls over and picks the cheque up from the bedside table, looks at it happily and kisses it. He then lies back, picks up the newspaper from the floor and starts to read it.

> ANGELA
> Well, it's alright for you. But I DO have to go to work.

> NORMAN
> What already?

> ANGELA
> Yes, it's gone ten. I`ll be late as it is.

ANGELA gets up and quickly dresses. She puts on a white nurses-style uniform and kisses NORMAN on the forehead.

>ANGELA
>See you later darling. Have a nice morning.

>NORMAN (still reading paper)
>Hmmm

>ANGELA
>We can go back to bed again when I get back if you like – before the kids get home from school…

We hear her footsteps going downstairs. Norman looks up, thinks to himself and calls out.

>NORMAN
>Don't forget to put your coat on!

>ANGELA (voice from downstairs)
>But it's such a lovely day

>NORMAN
>If anyone sees you're going to work we'll be right In the shit…

>ANGELA
>Ok darling, see you later.

Front door slams shut. Car is heard outside driving away. NORMAN goes back to reading paper.

Scene 21: INT- LIVING ROOM – DAY

NORMAN is on the telephone. In front of him on the table is a box of papers that he has obviously been sorting through.

NORMAN
Ah Baz! Bout time…I've been on hold for ages. These phone calls cost you know…!

We hear sounds of another person – a man talking - on the other end of the phone.

NORMAN
Well the bad news is that the deeds aren't anywhere to be found. No, no, I've looked through all her stuff. We went up to that revolting home for senile old grannies and I went through all her drawers whilst she was showing Angela the gardens – yes really.

NORMAN
Look, Baz. Why can't we do the same as with the old house and put in a statutory declaration that she is the legal owner – it worked before.

Scene switches to a solicitor's office. All very fine looking with dark oak shelves holding lots of old books. At a big luxurious desk sits a man in his mid 40s with greying hair and glasses wearing a navy blue pinstripe suit.

BAZ
Yes but don't forget that your wife has now assumed power of attorney. You remember - we managed to persuade that doctor to confirm that poor old Margie-Pargie was incapable of looking after herself - so that you and your empty headed ballet prancer could send her off to a home and spend all her money for her …

Scene alternates between NORMAN s living room and BAZ's office to follow the conversation.

NORMAN
Hey, now come on Baz, you got your new bloody car
out of it didn't you – you can't say it was all us.

BAZ
Anyway, the point that I'm trying to get at is that you
can't says she's lost her marbles one minute and
then decide the next that she's sane enough to
swear a declaration that she owns some bloody
property in London – just so you can sell it.

She's either senile or she isn't - gettit?

NORMAN
So we can't sell the bonds?

BAZ
Not unless you can drag out of her where she put the
certificates.

NORMAN
Maybe she gave them to the other daughter –
poncey bloody Lucy – to keep them out of sight -
what d'you reckon?

BAZ
Worth a try I suppose. You do seem to have a
fixation that her dad left her all the family fortune
when he popped off , don't you.

Tell you what, why don't I write her a letter accusing
of stealing the deeds to the shops and trying to
make money out of her poor old mum? That'll shake
her up a bit. She might even send us 'em back.

NORMAN
OK Baz. Give it a go. I'll check out the furniture in
storage one last time – you never know... Speak to
you soon. Love to Cheryl and the kids..

NORMAN puts the phone down and sits back in his chair, looking pensive.

                    NORMAN
                    Damnit! I always thought I`d married the wrong
                    sister...

Scene 22: EXT – CHURCHYARD – DAY

A very grim looking scene in the north Yorkshire moors. It is cloudy, raining and windy. A funeral service has just finished and the mourners are leaving. ANGELA , dressed in black and wiping back a few tears walks away from the grave yard. She sees her sister about to go out of the gate and runs to catch up with her…

>ANGELA
>Loo! Loo ! ooh do wait please… I hoped you'd come..

A well dressed and red eyed LUCY turns and hugs her sister.

>LUCY
>I almost missed it. The map that the car hire firm gave me didn't have this godforsaken place on it. So when I finally made it, I stood at the back so as not to disrupt things. I suppose nasty Norman's here somewhere about..

>ANGELA
>Er, I've left him.

>LUCY
>Oh again – how long for this time I wonder…

>ANGELA
>No, this time it's for good, I`ll tell you about it later. Have you got a car? I don't want to stay here – his family live nearby I'm sure they'll be looking for me – please, can we go..?

The pair get into a big shiny car parked just outside the church wall and drive off. As they drive away from the church, NORMAN s Volvo arrives. ANGELA ducks her head down so that he doesn't see her. NORMAN and LUCY exchange glares as they pass.

Scene 23: INT – TEA SHOP – DAY

LUCY and ANGELA are sitting at a table in the corner. ANGELA is sobbing, with her head in her hands. LUCY is trying to console her.

> LUCY
> But you never called me... I had no idea where you were. I `d have helped, you know I would have...

> ANGELA
> It all just went so wrong.... And then Mummy died and I couldn't take it any more... what am I going to do?

> LUCY
> And while you were sunning yourselves in Spain, you sent mummy to this place? No wonder she died. Must have died of rage I should think....

> ANGELA
> Oh Loo, don't be angry . It all seemed for the best at the time, She was getting very forgetful and it was so hard to look after her....I couldn't manage it any more.

> LUCY
> Well, now you're away from Norman you can get yourself sorted out once and for all.

> ANGELA
> Ooh, I couldn't manage on my own...

> LUCY
> Well look, there's the money from the sale of daddy's house. You could use some of that to put a deposit on somewhere nice, away from Norman and you could make a new start just you and the kids...

ANGELA looks sheepish, looks around in hesitation then grabs hold of LUCYs hands across the table.

ANGELA
That's just it, there isn't any money left…

LUCY
No, no, there's about 80.000 from the house plus mummy's own savings plus, she wouldn't have needed to touch that because of her income, so …..

ANGELA
Lucy – there's no money left. It's all gone. We bought some property in Spain … it got repossessed.

ANGELA collapses across the table in more tears. LUCY pulls her hands away and sits as if in a state of shock.

LUCY
I don't believe I'm hearing this! You mean all the money from the house – our family home - has been wasted?!?! …half of that was supposed to be mine. You know daddy always said to treat both daughters the same…

ANGELA
I'm sorry. It wasn't meant to turn out this way. It was going to be great, you could have come too… it was supposed to be for the good of everyone…

LUCY
So what happened? Tell me exactly…

ANGELA
Oh I don't know--- Norman said ….

LUCY
Norman, Norman , bloody Norman! why ever did you let him have mummy's savings…?

ANGELA
Lucy – it was impossible really, you had to be there to know…

LUCY
Yes, if I`d have been there I`d have put a stop to it. That's obviously why no-one told me where to find you…

ANGELA
We ought to go. My train's at 4 and I feel uncomfortable around here. Norman's spies might tell him I'm here..

LUCY
So where are you staying?

ANGELA
Me and the kids are staying with my friend Maureen in Bradford just for now. I'm going to the housing people to find use somewhere permanent.

Scene 24: EXT – RAILWAY PLATFORM – DAY

LUCY and ANGELA are standing awkwardly waiting for the train to arrive.

> LUCY
> Look if you really are stuck for money, I've still got that thousand pounds that mummy gave me. You remember she gave us both some.

ANGELA seems to brighten up a bit and throws her arms around LUCY in a big hug.

> ANGELA
> Oh, I KNEW you'd still have yours…!

Before things can go any further, the train pulls into the station. LUCY doesn't rush to give ANGELA any money as she had hoped so ANGELA climbs onto the train.

> LUCY
> Write and tell me where you're living. You've got my address in Geneva…

The train pulls out. ANGELA waves until she is out of sight. LUCY takes a deep breath, trying to take in what she has learnt. She fights back a few tears then walks off the platform in the direction of the car park.

Scene 25: INT – Lucy`s LIVING ROOM – EVENING

LUCY is sitting in a luxurious armchair with a cup of tea on the table beside her. She looks pensive as she makes jottings with a pen and paper.

> LUCY
> So that's 80.000 from the house – plus the savings mummy had – say another 10.000 - then the rental income that mummy had when she was living with them, hmm I bet she didn't see too much of that.
>
> Over 6 years that's   oh my god… its nearly 150.000 pounds they've managed to get through…. And half of that was supposed to be mine…!
>
> Then she had the audacity to try and scrounge that thousand pounds that mummy gave me…just because she had spent hers….
>
> Bloody unbelievable….!.I couldn't do that to anyone…

There is a sudden ring at the door. LUCY slowly puts her pad down and goes to the spy hole. Then quickly unlocks and opens the doors. A flamboyantly dressed black man is standing outside. His face lights up as he sees LUCY .

> BRADFORD
> Lucy Gordon my soul sister! So you are here after all!

LUCY throws her arms around Bradford

> LUCY
> Bradford! It's great to see you. I didn't even know you were coming to Switzerland. You should have called…

BRADFORD
I've been calling all day, Sis, but you weren't home...

They go into the living room. LUCY puts Bradford's coat on a hanger.

LUCY
So what are you doing in Switzerland – and how long
are you here...?

BRADFORD
Questions, questions – you always were the nosey
one weren't you...

LUCY
Oh, come on, don't tease ... tell me...

BRADFORD
Ok, Ok, well you know that I'm now regional director
for Danceworks in Europe...

LUCY
I didn't know that – congratulations

BRADFORD
Well, you do now... anyway, I'm currently setting up
a new European tour for an American troupe for next
summer and doing the rounds looking at theatres,
hotels and so on...

LUCY
And that's why you're in Geneva – how fabulous..

BRADFORD
No that` s not it! Let me finish, will you....

LUCY
Oh, I'm sorry, I keep butting in, it's just so great to
see you again – when was the last time? Mummy's
birthday party, I think when she had that huge
cake......?

BRADFORD
I'm not in Geneva for Danceworks. I was down in Chamonix at the Ice Palace but I came here especially to see you. It's important, it's Angie.

LUCY
Angie? what's wrong with her? I only saw a week ago, she was fine then, well a bit down really as it was....

BRADFORD
Mummy's funeral, yes I know. I cried when I heard.

LUCY
But she told me that she had left Norman and was going to sort herself out.

BRADFORD
Well, she's back with Norman and deep in the do-do if you ask me...

LUCY
You've seen her?

BRADFORD
Just three days ago – and she wasn't a happy bunny, I can tell you.
LUCY
But if she's in trouble why didn't she call me..?

BRADFORD
Something to do with money and a house? Anyway, she said you didn't love her anymore and wouldn't help her..... or something like that...

LUCY
Rubbish, anyway how come she's back with Norman...?

BRADFORD
Well, from the sound of it, he tracked her down to the
place she was holed up – followed the kids home
from school, I think. Then he made such a fuss that
the friend she was stopping with said she couldn't
stay there no more...

So that was it, game over – she went rushing back to
Nasty Norman.

I was doing rehearsals for backing dancers at the
Odsall Empire on Thursday and there she was,
interviewing for a cleaning job.

LUCY
Cleaning – oh no...

BRADFORD
Hey that's not the worst of it either. That Norman's
had her out doing all sorts of rotten jobs and then
he's claiming benefit at the same time. Ever since
they got back from Spain , he just sits around
reading the paper and boozing all her money away
then expects her to cook clean and the rest when
she gets home.

LUCY
Poor Angela, she didn't tell me any of that when I
saw her..

BRADFORD
Well, I tried to help her. I couldn't take her on as a
dancer cuz she's... er, well, she's not as young as
the rest of the line up but I said I`d try and get her a
supervisor's job with the theatre bosses when I talk
to them next week.

LUCY
So will you see Angie next week as well? I haven't
got her phone number or address or anything.

BRADFORD
Just as well, Norman is checking all calls and letters.
He wants to make sure she don't get away again.

Scene 26: INT – NORMAN & ANGELAS BEDROOM – DAY

NORMAN is dozing in bed, two or three days` papers are thrown around on the floor and last night's whisky bottle stands empty on the bedside table. ANGELA is creeping around trying not to be heard and getting dressed to go out. NORMAN suddenly wakes up.

> NORMAN
> Oi, where are you sneaking off to so early in the morning?

> ANGELA
> I'm not sneaking anywhere, Just didn't want to wake you that's all. Anyway it's gone ten - not early at all.

> NORMAN
> Gone ten? So what happened to my bloody breakfast eh? A bloke needs proper sustenance after a night of passion you know.

ANGELA winces and raises her hand to feel some fresh looking bruising on the left side of her face

> ANGELA (under breath)
> Don't remind me…

> ANGELA (loudly)
> Anyway, I've got to back to the theatre today, they want me for a second interview…I did tell you…

> NORMAN
> What for a cleaning job? They do second interviews… you are joking

> ANGELA
> No, er they've asked me to go back ….anyway we do need the money.

NORMAN
Too right we do. That money from your mum's
properties ain't enough to keep a cat alive bloody
cheek if you ask me. Anyway, don't be late back…
I've managed to get you a couple of shifts at the pub
– starting this lunchtime.

ANGELA *curses inwardly to herself, puts her jacket on and heads*
down stairs.

NORMAN (shouting after her)
Bring me the mail up before you go. On second
thoughts I`ll come and get it, make sure nothing goes
astray…

Scene 27: *EXT – STREET SCENE OUSIDE THEATRE – DAY*

From a distance we see BRADFORD standing waiting outside the theatre. Pacing up and down and looking at his watch. Then ANGELA goes up to him, they hug and disappear inside.

Scene 28: *INT – THEATRE CAFE - DAY*

BRADFORD and ANGELA are sitting in a corner of the cafe, which otherwise appears to be shut.

>   ANGELA
> But I can't leave him.. I've told you – he won't let me go…and what about all my things…?
>
>   BRADFORD
> I told you, Lucy said she'd help. She's given me some money for you, you could fly to Switzerland right now…
>
>   ANGELA
> Anyway, I couldn't possibly go anywhere until Sonya starts away at University next term… I don't want to leave her on her own with him..
>
>   BRADFORD
> Come on she's a big girl – eighteen is she, she can look after herself
>
>   ANGELA
> No, I must stay for Sonya's sake. That's all I can say.
>
>   BRADFORD
> OK, well it's up to you. But do ring Lucy and let her know what's going on, she's really worried about you.

ANGELA
Well, Ok I`ll…

BRADFORD (*handing her an envelope*)
Look here's the money she gave me, you keep it until you need to use it..

ANGELA (*pushes the money back*)
No, don't give it to me. If Norman finds it he'll only spend it and hit me for keeping it from him..

BRADFORD
Ok, well if you won't take the money, take this phone number and keep it safe. When you decide to get away give this guy a call and mention my name. He'll give you all the help he can.. he's OK, he's a mate

BRADFORD hands ANGELA a business card bearing the name Ace Security Services. She looks sceptical but puts it into her purse. She looks at her watch and gets up to go.

ANGELA
I really must dash. Norman's got me a job in his rotten pub. It wouldn't be so bad but I bet he'll be there drinking all my wages before I even get them… that cleaning job would've helped…

BRADFORD
Hey - yes, I was going to tell you about that! I had a word with the manager of the dry cleaners across the road. They do all the costumes for here. He said you should pop in and see him on your way past.

ANGELA
Oh Bradders, you are an angel! Thanks so much for everything. Gotta go..!

BRADFORD
Hey, Bradford Yorkes at your service…!

ANGELA gives BRADFORD a big hug and rushes off. BRADFORD looks out of the window to watch her go. He sees her cross the road and look in the window of the dry cleaners. She hesitates for a moment before going in. BRADFORD smiles to himself and leaves the cafe.

Scene 29: INT – PUB BAR - DAY

It's a fairly rowdy lunchtime session and one barman is struggling to keep the customers at bay. NORMAN is sitting at the bar looking into his glass and then at the clock and back again. The clock says 12.10

ANGELA rushes in taking her coat off as she does and makes for behind the bar - a sarcastic cheer comes from the bar customers.

> NORMAN
> Where the bloody hell have you been? We need this job, you know…

> ANGELA
> I'm sorry – sorry John – got held up. Had an interview at the dry cleaners - said he'll let me know…

> NORMAN
> Dry cleaners? What about the theatre cleaning job? Don't you dare go wandering off without telling me…

ANGELA glares at him and starts serving other customers.

> NORMAN
> Ere, Luv stick us a pint in there will you. Should get it cheaper now we're staff shouldn't we…

> ANGELA
> Huh, not much "we" about it from where I'm standing..

ANGELA pulls NORMAN a very frothy pint and bangs it down on the counter so that it splashes over him. She goes to the other end of the bar to serve other customers.

Another look at the clock. Time goes by it is now 2.30.

NORMAN
Oh well, darling. Just another half hour then you'll be
finished. Then we can go home and have some
lunch – what are you cooking anyway…?.

The clock now says 3.00.

ANGELA
Right, finished thank god…I`ll get my coat…

NORMAN (a little drunk)
Bout time and all…. Give us your purse I`ll get some
fags..

*ANGELA picks her handbag up from behind the counter and goes to
take per purse out but NORMAN dips his hand in and snatches it out*

NORMAN
It's alright - I`ll do it. You get ready to go. I'm bloody
starving!

*ANGELA goes to get her coat but then remembers that the Private
detectives card is in her purse. She looks back and watches
NORMAN in horror as he opens her purse and starts slowly fishing
about for change.*

NORMAN
Not much in here is there? You been nipping off for
cream teas again or what?

ANGELA
No, I er – oh here let me do it.

Tension mounts and ANGELA tries to grab her purse back.

NORMAN
Ah, here we are - a fiver hidden away you naughty
thing!

*NORMAN takes the money and idly throws the purse back at
ANGELA . She grasps it close to her and breathes a sigh of relief.*

Slowly and slyly she goes back behind the bar, carefully watching NORMAN s every move as he tries to work the cigarette machine.

When she is certain he is not looking, she slips the business card from her purse and pins it up on the board next to the end of the bar, hidden among all the other business cards that people have put there.

> NORMAN (*cheerful with cigarette in mouth*)
> So, we off now then? What are you doing, not looking for another job surely..?
>
> (*he jokes to listening public*)
> Workaholic this woman is ... see you lads tomorrow, eh..?

ANGELA rushes out of the pub, NORMAN saunters behind her saying goodbye to all sorts of people as he leaves.

Scene 30: *MONTAGE SCENE*

Showing the passage of time and the drudgery that ANGELA has to suffer. Background music for this sequence is "Brittle" by The Meantime . On the screen we see alternating shots of

- *Calendar pages being torn off to show passing of each month*
- *ANGELA working at the dry cleaners*
- *ANGELA pulling pints and looking wistfully at the detective's card on the pub board*
- *ANGELA cooking and cleaning at home*
- *NORMAN lounging around shouting at her*

Final shot of the sequence is ANGELA picking up the mail one morning and calling to SONYA who comes and opens the letter. SONYA jumps with delight and hugs ANGELA. Her exam grades are good enough to get to University.

Scene 31: INT – PUB BAR - EVENING

It is now late summer. ANGELA is working the evening shift in the pub. NORMAN is hovering around in the background as usual. This evening, ANGELA looks very restless. She snatches an opportunity to take the card from the board when NORMAN goes to the toilet.

> NORMAN
> Alright darling, how's the head now?

> ANGELA
> Oh, a little better now, now the sun's come out. It seems to have brightened everywhere up again..

> NORMAN
> Stick a pint in there will you love?

NORMAN slides his glass across the counter. ANGELA takes it and fills it up.

> ANGELA
> Didn't I see you talking to Bill earlier?

> NORMAN
> You certainly did – with a bit of luck he's going to put a bit of business my way
> (he looks up) oh, there he is, out in the garden - I`ll just go and have a quick word….

ANGELA grabs her chance. She goes to the payphone around the corner of the bar and dials the number on the card, watching NORMAN through the window as she does. She waits for a moment as she waits for an answer.

> ANGELA
> Oh, hello.. is that erm Ace erm
>
> It is? Oh good. Listen, a Mr Yorkes gave me your number ages ago   Bradford yes… that's me Mrs no no its Davison – only one D

Well, I really can't talk freely at the moment. Can we meet?

Could you come here tomorrow lunch time to the pub I'm working at?

ANGELA sees NORMAN finish his conversation through the window. He turns to come back into the bar room

Yes, that would be best.. see you then must go....

NORMAN
Well that went OK then…

ANGELA (*nervously*)
What did? What you mean?

NORMAN
With Bill, you daft woman, what were we just talking about?

ANGELA
Oh yes, of course, what's happening then?

NORMAN
Well, I shouldn't say too much yet

NORMAN draws closer and begins to whisper

NORMAN
Stick another pint in would you darling..? anyway yes, Bill knows someone who goes abroad a lot – you know courier vans to the continent. Well, he reckons that you can buy booze and fags really cheap over there if you know where to go and then sell 'em back here at a huge profit. He says he'll bring us a share next time he goes...

ANGELA
But that's illegal surely....

NORMAN
No more illegal then you working whilst I'm claiming
unemployment benefit for you. You'd better watch
your step my girl or you'll be in trouble with the social

ANGELA
What me? It's you that's making the claims.....you
don't think they'd come after me do you..?

NORMAN
Not if you leave it all to me, my darling. Now don't
you worry your pretty little head about any more
complicated things like that.

Give us a pint for Bill will you, I'll go and firm things
up with him...

Scene 32: INT – PUB BAR - DAY

ANGELA is serving behind the bar. Every time someone opens the door she jumps and looks to see who it is. The man known as Bill comes up to the bar and orders a drink.

> BILL
> Isn't Norm in today? He's normally here every lunchtime...

> ANGELA
> Well, he said he'd got a bit of an upset stomach after last night....

> BILL
> Huh, last night he promised faithfully he'd bring me some money for our little business deal....

> ANGELA (*under her breath*)
> That's obviously why he's not here then....
> (*openly*)
> oh did he...? I`ll remind him later...

ANGELA carries on serving other people and looking around. A short while later one of the customers sitting at the bar waves ANGELA over, leans across the counter and whispers to her. He is very non-descript looking and blends very well with the surroundings.

> PHIL (*cautiously*)
> Are you Mrs Davidson...?

> ANGELA (*still looking around*)
> Yes, well Davison – just one D.

> PHIL
> You called me yesterday.... Mr Yorkes contact?

> ANGELA
> What you...? a private detec.....

PHIL
SSSh not so loud...
Don't want to attract too much attention...can we
talk..?

ANGELA (*checks where the other barman is...*)
Yes, come round the back. The landlord's popped
out for a while.

*ANGELA motions to PHIL to go round the corner which leads behind
the bar to the hallway beyond. PHIL slips through and ANGELA
follows him.*

ANGELA

Sorry about that. I've been on tenterhooks all
morning. I didn't expect you to look like that... .

PHIL

What like a normal person? What did you expect – a
big hat and a long coat like on the telly? I think not.

ANGELA
Well ,of course, I

PHIL

I tell you – if everyone can tell you're a private
investigator then the job's blown. Gotta blend in
.......So, I'm taking you to the airport right...?

ANGELA

Oh are you? Oh god it's all so sudden...I`ll er have to
get a few things together and then tell Mr Chadwick
that I won't be in at the cleaners....

PHIL

First thing is – you don't tell anyone you're going.
Otherwise word`ll get round and you won't get away
– OK?

ANGELA
Right, OK. Don't tell anyone – right

PHIL
You don't pack too much stuff otherwise it'll be noticed at home. Just one bag and a small case if you can keep it hidden.

ANGELA
One case, OK

PHIL
I`ll pick you up at 4pm tomorrow. Your house is third from the end, right, I`ll wait round the corner. It's a blue escort. I`ll give your phone 3 rings when I'm in position. If everything's OK, don't answer, just come...

PHIL slips away back to the bar room. ANGELA stands thinking to herself trying to remember what he has said. ANGELA follows him out

ANGELA
Was that a blue....??

ANGELA looks out across the bar. PHIL has gone.

Scene 33: INT – LIVING ROOM - DAY

ANGELA is rushing around the house picking up ornaments, putting them down, picking them up again and trying to cram as much as she can in several medium sized cases. The telephone rings. She almost jumps out of her skin. She goes to answer it, then leaves it. She counts three rings and the phone stops. She looks agitatedly out of the window then carries on rushing round, trying to pack

Another quick look at the clock. It now says 10 past 4. ANGELA still isn't ready. The doorbell rings. She jumps. Looks out of the window. Opens the door. PHIL is standing there, holding a clipboard bearing the name of a cable TV company.

> PHIL
> Mrs Davidson - everything OK?

> ANGELA
> Oh, er ....we don't want cable .....thank you

ANGELA goes to shut the door. PHIL rams his foot in and looks her straight in the face.

> PHIL
> Mrs Davidson! It's me, Phil ....

> ANGELA
> Ooh, sorry I thought you were the TV man ....

> PHIL (*sighing*)
> When you didn't come out on time. I thought I`d better come and see if everything was OK – this is a **disguise**.... Where's your husband.? Is he about?

> ANGELA
> No, he went to see his bookmaker, er bookie, earlier but I'm worried he might come back now the racing's finished.

PHIL
In that case we'd better make a move. Come on, I`ll
take your bag.

ANGELA
Yes, OK, they're just in here…

PHIL follows ANGELA into the living room. She points to her pile of cases as she carries on filling another one.

PHIL
I told you, one shoulder bag and a small case…..
what are we going to do with all this lot

ANGELA
Yes, but what about all my things….there's my
photos, my ballet stuff, my ornaments, all mummy's
jugs….

PHIL
This is supposed to be a covert escape operation.
There's no way we can leave unobserved if you're
insisting on taking all this luggage. Now two cases –
no more, Mrs Davidson.

ANGELA
It's Davison – just one "d" – oh who cares, it's his
name anyway – call me Angela – it's easier….just
two cases? oh dear…..

Sounds of key being put in front door. Glance towards front door. Silhouette of NORMAN visible through glass trying to fit his key in the lock.

ANGELA
Oh no! It's Norman. He's back!

PHIL
Right, time to go…can we get out the back?

ANGELA
Yes, through the garden.....

PHIL
You go and get into the car – the keys are in it. I`ll try
and hold him off for a while. You drive off and I`1ll
meet you at the end of the road…

ANGELA
But he's a trained killer. He was in special forces in
Cyprus

PHIL
Oh, that's different then, c`mon!

*PHIL grabs one of the cases in one hand and takes ANGELA s arm
in the other and pulls her towards the kitchen. As she leaves the
living room, she just manages to grab her handbag.*

The front door finally opens.

NORMAN
Hi darling! Norm's home.… Angela?

*ANGELA disappears out the back door. PHIL pushes the kitchen
table in front of the inner door to slow down any pursuit. NORMAN
sees the abandoned cases in the living room and, hearing the noise
in the kitchen, goes to investigate.*

*He goes to open the door to the kitchen but it is stuck. He pushes
hard against it and it moves a little bit. He gives an almighty shove
and the doors slides to half open, wedged with the kitchen table
behind it. He squeezes himself through the gap, scrambles over the
table and bounds over to the open back door, just in time to see
PHIL shoving ANGELA through the hedge at the end of the garden.*

*Switch to other side of hedge. PHIL is dragging ANGELA through the
hedge. Her cardigan gets snagged up, he gives an almighty tug and
the hedge gives way, leaving them both in a heap on the pavement.*

PHIL
Come on, get up.....

PHIL picks up ANGELA and the bags and drags her round the corner to where the car is parked.

ANGELA (*out of breath, trying to keep up*)
Do you think he saw us....?

PHIL
Most likely.

PHIL throws the bags onto the back seat. Angela gets in the passenger side. PHIL jumps in the car and starts the engine. The car speeds away with a skid and a roar. As it rounds the corner, NORMAN is seen rushing out of the front door, gesticulating wildly.

Scene 34: INT – INSIDE CAR - DAY

The car is parked behind a parade of shops. PHIL is stretching back in his seat with a rather relieved look. ANGELA is sitting weeping in the passenger seat.

          PHIL
          Well, that could have been worse…!

          ANGELA
          Worse? How could it be? All my things, they're still in the house, Ill never be able to get them now….

          PHIL
          Don't worry about them. We'll get them later… the most important thing now is to get you to the airport…

          ANGELA
          Oh, no , I've ….er… changed my mind…..I can't go through with it…

          PHIL
          You don't want to go back **<u>there</u>**…**<u>now</u>** ?

          ANGELA
          No, I couldn't, I really couldn't… oh what am I going to do…?

          PHIL
          You're going to the damned airport, like I've been paid for…. OK?

ANGELA nods reluctantly and collapses into more floods of tears. PHIL fastens his seatbelt, starts the car and they drive off.

Scene 35: INT – AIRPORT - DAY

Busy airport terminal. PHIL is looking around trying to find out where ANGELA needs to go. She is in the magazine shop buying things for the flight. PHIL comes to hurry her along.

> PHIL
> Come on, the plane's about to board, You've got to check in NOW

> ANGELA
> Have you found the check in?

> PHIL
> Yes, it's the one at the end, now come on…

As they come out of the magazine shop, ANGELA s face drops. She darts back in and motions to PHIL to follow.

> PHIL
> Bloody hell, what is it now?

> ANGELA
> It's Norman – he's there…!

> PHIL
> I told you not to get paranoid, so far you've seen him in 5 different places since we left your place… he was at the petrol station, he was operating the car park barrier he was….

> ANGELA
> No but this time it really is him, look!

The pair of them look through the wire shelves of a magazine stand. NORMAN is standing in the middle of the departure hall talking to an Airport security officer, blocking the way to the departure gate. They are both looking around.

> PHIL
> Does he know that security guy?

ANGELA
Well, don't forget he's ex-Army – most of his old
mates have gone into security firms...

PHIL
That's blown it. There's no way you can get checked
in for the flight now...how did he know to look
here....

ANGELA
Well, er I ......

PHIL
Go on, spit it out...

ANGELA
He must have read the luggage tags on the bags we
left behind, I told you we should have brought them
with us...

PHIL
Luggage tags? You mean you made us late cuz you
were writing luggage tags..? God, this just gets
worse....

ANGELA
What are going to do now?

PHIL
How the hell should I know? Best get back to the car
I suppose....
Come on, and keep your head down.

*The pair of them sneak away from the departure area and cautiously
make their way back to the car park.*

Scene 36: EXT - CAR - DAY

*PHIL's car is parked behind a parade of rough looking shops. He is
sitting in the drivers seat looking annoyed and staring straight ahead.
ANGELA is sitting in the passenger seat in floods of tears.*

> PHIL
> I should leave you here you know…forget the whole
> thing.

> ANGELA (sobbing)
> I'm sorry – it's not my fault

PHIL swings round to look at her

> PHIL
> Yes it is – it's all your bloody fault. You didn't follow
> any of the instructions I gave you. Fancy leaving
> luggage tags and cases laying around – even a
> complete idiot might just work out you were going
> away somewhere…

> ANGELA (*still sobbing*)
> What are we going to do now

> PHIL
> Well, we can't really go back to the airport , it's not
> safe there. I could take you back to your house

ANGELA starts to wail again

> PHIL
> OK OK calm down , I'll think of something else. And
> DO stop crying, it makes it hard to think

> ANGELA
> That's just the sort of thing he would say…all you
> men are the same

> PHIL
> Oh look, I'm sorry…

HE puts his hand out to reassuringly touch her shoulder

> PHIL
> Really, I didn't mean to shout it's just with everything
> going wrong, I'm a bit stressed out that's all.

ANGELA cheers up a bit, stops sniffling and rests her head on his shoulder.

> ANGELA
> So what do you suggest we do?

> PHIL
> OK how's this sound…
>
> There's the travel agents just up the road where I go
> the flight tickets from. I could go and cash them in
> and we could the money to drive through the tunnel
> and get out that way.
>
> It might give us a bit of headstart if your husband
> still thinks we'll be trying to fly out. Even if he's got
> some of his mates looking out for us, they might not
> be watching Folkestone too closely.

ANGELA sits up straight in a determined manner and wipes away the remaining tears

> ANGELA
> Right – let's do it. Drive on!

They exchange a brief smile and PHIL starts the car and they drive off up the road.

Scene 37: INT - LUCY's FLAT - NIGHT

ANGELA and PHIL are sat on LUCY's sofa with blankets round their shoulders and warm drinks cupped in their hands. They have obviously had a long and tiring trip as Angela's hair is untidy and her make up has faded. ANGELA has been telling the story so far.

ANGELA
... and that's how we got here.

LUCY
Wow, what a story! Do you do this sort of thing often, Mr Banks?

PHIL
Not really, Miss er Gordon , no. Do call me Phil, please.

LUCY
Thank you Phil. Please call me Lucy.

PHIL
Right, er Lucy. No it's normally following people for divorce cases, tracing lost puppies that sort of thing.

ANGELA
And Bradders paid for you to come and rescue me- how wonderful..!

PHIL (*sheepishly*)
Yes, well, it's not quite as simple as that.

LUCY
Why's that then?

PHIL
Well, Mr Yorkes said that **you** would be paying my bill upon safe delivery of your sister, Miss Gordon, - I mean, Lucy.

LUCY
Did he indeed..? Well we'll sort that out in the
morning I think. It's very late and I really must go to
bed.

ANGELA (standing up)
Ooh yes I think I'll turn in too…I suppose I get the
spare room do I?
And Phil can have the settee..

She leaves the room, calling out as she goes

I can borrow some pjs can't I, Loo….night all...

*PHIL and LUCY smile at each other. PHIL shrugs and helps LUCY
with blankets and pillows to make up the sofa.*

Scene 38: INT - LUCY's FLAT - MORNING

ANGELA is making herself some breakfast in the kitchen wearing a dressing gown that is much too big for her. PHIL comes in wearing shorts and vest. He obviously didn't sleep very well.

> PHIL
> Morning – has Lucy gone out..?
>
> ANGELA
> Yes she had to go into work – terrible bore really – tea?
>
> PHIL (*sitting down at the table*)
> Yes, please.
>
> ANGELA (*also sits down*)
> It's in the pot if you want it.
>
> PHIL
> Charming…

He gets up, pours himself some tea and puts some bread in the toaster

> PHIL
> So what are , you going to do now, now you're here and safe from Norman..?
>
> ANGELA
> Don't know – relax for a while I suppose. Get myself sorted out – find a job, place of my own.
>
> PHIL
> Can, you speak Swiss then?
>
> ANGELA
> Silly, there's no such thing as Swiss! They speak French and German in most of the country and around here is a German bit.

The toaster pops. PHIL gets up and brings the toast to the table. He sits down and butters the toast.

          PHIL *(offering ANGELA some toast)*
          So you do speak German then?

          ANGELA
          Jawohl - mein Herr! I'll have you know I was top of
          the bill at the Berlin Ballet from nineteen sixty…er…
          seventy .. well, for quite a while, you know!

She takes a piece of his toast and proceeds to remove most of the butter from it with her knife before munching on it.

          PHIL
          Wow, a real star in our midst. So what happened.

          ANGELA
          What do you mean what happened?

          PHIL
          Well, how did the dazzling star of the Berlin Ballet
          end up married to an alcoholic layabout in Bradford?

ANGELA snaps out of her flippant flirty mood and seems taken aback at the question

          ANGELA
          I'd rather not talk about it to be honest…

          PHIL
          Whoops, hit a wrong note obviously.

PHIL gets up from the table and goes to leave the kitchen.

          ANGELA *(changing the subject)*
          What will you do now?

          PHIL
          I'll have to get back to England - got jobs waiting for
          me.

PHIL sticks his head back round the door

>**PHIL**
>Hey - wouldn't it be funny if your Norman hired me to try and find you..?

>**ANGELA**
>Not really, to be honest - you wouldn't tell him, would you?

PHIL comes back into the kitchen and tries to tease her

>**PHIL**
>If he hired me then I'd have to do what he said

ANGELA begins to get upset

>**ANGELA**
>But what about me? You're supposed to be protecting me.. I'm your little damson in distress and you rescued me.

She looks as if she is about to burst into tears. She takes a step towards PHIL, stumbles and falls against him very dramatically. He puts his arms around here and she makes sobbing noises against his chest.

>**PHIL**
>Don't worry, I won't let him find you - I'll look after you.

Scene 39: INT- HALLWAY - DAY

LUCY arrives home from work, carrying her briefcase and some groceries. She opens the door and comes through grasping the packages.

>LUCY
>Angie! I'm back. Thought I'd bring some lunch home and have it with you.

LUCY goes through to the kitchen and starts unpacking the shopping, still calling out as she goes.

>LUCY
>Has Phil gone already? I'll have to send him a cheque I suppose. Nice bloke really. I've also bought some spare toiletries I know how you like to have your own brands.

She looks around. Still no sign of ANGELA. Her gaze fixes on the still closed spare bedroom door.

>LUCY (*to herself*)
>Poor kid must be exhausted after all that excitement

She goes to the spare bedroom and quietly opens the door. Through the crack in the door we see ANGELA and PHIL naked in bed together - both fast asleep. LUCY quickly closes the door again.

>LUCY (*to herself*)
>Definitely exhausted…

LUCY picks up her coat and her bag and goes back out to work.

Scene 40 INT – LUCY's FLAT – NIGHT

It is now several days later. The flat looks rather untidy and LUCY is obviously annoyed that PHIL and ANGIE are making themselves very much at home, leaving her to clear up the mess they have made.

The three of them are sitting at the dining table for the evening meal.

> LUCY
> I don't wish this to sound rude, Phil, but how long were you thinking of staying..?

PHIL and ANGELA have obviously been spending a lot of time together and have built up lots of little private jokes and mannerisms which does not help the situation.

> ANGELA (*in a childish voice*)
> Oh Loo, he can't go - he's looking after me…

> PHIL (*sipping wine – a little too much*)
> Absolutely – and it's all going on the bill, I can tell you!

> LUCY
> Don't keep on about your bill. I have told you more than once that I will settle your account in full and in cash as soon as you give me an itemised list of charges and expenses - and not before!

PHIL looks down at his plate.

> PHIL
> Oh come on, I've already explained that to you. Angie decided to put my clothes in the washer – they wiff a bit and I haven't got a change with me - and all the receipts and stuff got washed. , You didn't want me to go around in dirty clothes did you?

ANGELA giggles and goes to make a silly comment but LUCY give her a fierce glance and she shuts up, also looking own into her plate with a mischievous grin on her face.

>LUCY
>Well , you'll just have to bill me for your time – from the moment you left Bradford until you arrived here and no more – OK?

>PHIL (*still looking at his plate*)
>Sure, I'll sort that out in the morning.

>LUCY
>I suppose you'll be ready to get off then, won't, you.

ANGELA picks up on the obscure double entendre and starts to giggle again. She gets up and rushes from the dining room in fits of laughter. PHIL tries to hide his smile. LUCY turns to face him.

>LUCY
>You really ought to be careful of Angie, you know.

>PHIL
>Hmm?

>LUCY
>She might be all over you now but she'll drop you as quick as anything if the mood takes her. Just don't get too attached.

>PHIL (*thinks about this and sobers up somewhat*)
>Right – thanks for erm telling me. You'll have that bill in the morning.
>I think I'll turn in now.

PHIL stands up and leaves the room. He hesitates outside ANGELA's bedroom door but instead of going in, goes into the living room and tarts making up the bed on the settee.

Scene 41: INT – LUCY's OFFICE - DAY

LUCY is working in her office at the bank. The door flies open and ANGELA comes in all excited.

> ANGELA
> You'll never guess what I've got

> LUCY
> Pregnant?

> ANGELA
> Oh don't be beastly – come on, guess…

> LUCY
> Look, Angie I'm supposed to be working here. Couldn't it wait until tonight?

> ANGELA
> Oh Loo, you're such a killjoy. I've got some really exciting news for you and I'm dying to tell you and all you can do is moan.

LUCY stands up from her desk, takes ANGELA's jacket from her and hangs it on the coast stand. She then guides her softly by the shoulders into an arm chair.

> LUCY
> Just let me finish this one sheet and then you can tell me all about it

LUCY sits back at her desk and is about to start work again when ANGELA chirps up again

> ANGELA
> You'll be excited too, I'm sure…

LUCY throws her a dirty look over the top of her reading glasses and carries on with her work.

After a few minutes of silence, ANGELA starts to get bored with sitting quietly and starts fidgeting on the chair, crossing and uncrossing her legs and then balancing her shoe on the end of her big toe and swinging it up and down.

ANGELA flicks her shoe up into the air with her toe. She goes to catch it again with her foot but kicks a little glass table that is next to the chair knocking over a water jug and breaking one of the four glasses.

LUCY slams down her pen and glares at ANGELA. ANGELA looks around in innocent surprise and a secretary throws open the office door to see what has happened.

LUCY stands up

> LUCY
> Its alright, Marlies – I'll deal with it.

LUCY ushers the secretary away and comes back with a dustpan and cloth. She cleans up the mess and then sits in another armchair giving ANGELA her full attention.

> LUCY
> Right what was it that was so important that you had to rush all the way here and tell me..?

> ANGELA
> Its Karl!

> LUCY
> Karl? Karl who?

> ANGELA
> My Karl!

> LUCY
> Your Karl, what about him?

> ANGELA
> I've found him!

LUCY
You never lost him. You left him as I recall…

ANGELA
Yes, but …

LUCY
First for Dieter…

ANGELA
But anyway…

LUCY
Then for Hans…

ANGELA
OK, but that wasn't…

LUCY
And then you just got back with him when you left
him again and married Norman..

ANGELA (*stands up, annoyed*)
Why do you have to bring all that up again. It's all in
the past! You know it makes me feel bad.

LUCY
Not half as bad as Karl felt, I'll be bound.
So, you've **found** him , you say….

ANGELA (*slumps back down in her chair again*)
Hmmf - don't know if I want to tell you now. You've
ruined the surprise.

*LUCY leans across in front of her sister, strokes her hair and pats
her on the back of the head as one would a child*

LUCY
OK, I'm sorry. Now come on - do tell me your news.

ANGELA (*sniffing back a pretend tear*)
Alright then, so long as you promise not to interrupt

LUCY (*sitting back in chair, crosses fingers to emphasise her words*)
Promise!

ANGELA forgets all her previous sulkiness and launches into her exciting tale

ANGELA
Well I was reading that film magazine of yours – the one , you had on the coffee table…….what's it called … ooh , you know…?

LUCY
Yes, but you told me not to interrupt..

ANGELA throws a tiresome glance at LUCY

LUCY
Ok its called "Deutche Film Woche"…get on with it…

ANGELA
Right, well I was flicking through it this morning, just before I was going to start the washing up that you had left me to do

LUCY
So, you didn't do it?

ANGELA
What…

LUCY
The washing up – you said , you were going to do it and then….

ANGELA
Yes, well, anyway, look don't interrupt! In the
magazine there was an interview with a Berlin film
director – Kurt somebody.

LUCY
So...?

ANGELA
Well, he's not important but the production company
that was making the film was called "Werner Erhardt
Film Production"

LUCY
And..?

ANGELA
Don't you see..? Werner Erhardt – Karl Erhardt –
Werner was - er - is Karl's brother – my Karl! So all
I've got to do is find the number for his firm in Berlin

LUCY
Didn't you run off with Werner once as well..?

ANGELA
Oh come on Loo, that didn't mean anything! Anyway
it was ages ago...
Can I use your office phone....?

LUCY
What? To ring your ex-boyfriend's brother who you
had a fling with before dumping him for his own
brother again so that , you can now out of the blue
ask him about his brother...after all these years..?
Yes I do mind...!

ANGELA (*jumping out of her chair in a sulk*)
You always were jealous of me – jealous of the fact
that men fancied me and not you – that I was
married and you weren't! You're still the same...!

ANGELA picks up her things and storms out of the office

> LUCY (*calling after her*)
> Angie – come back. Don't be silly

ANGELA can be seen marching out through the typing pool. She hurls open the door to the stairwell and flounces out.

> LUCY (*calling after her*)
> Don't forget the washing up…

LUCY stands speechless watching the wake that her sister has left as she stormed through the office. She sighs to herself in a resigned a manner and goes back to her work.

Scene 42: INT - LUCYS FLAT – NIGHT

It is early evening. The flat still looks rather untidy. In the background we see a huge mountain of washing up piled up in the kitchen. Phil has bought a big bunch of flowers that is laying still wrapped on one of the armchairs. He is humming to himself and seems very pleased with himself. From one of the numerous carrier bags he pulls some slinky underwear and holds it up to the light.

We hear the jingle of keys and the front door bang. PHIL holds the underwear up in front of him and goes towards the hall.

> PHIL
> Angie – look what I found in ……

Instead of ANGELA, LUCY walks in carrying her briefcase and overcoat. PHIL's face drops and he quickly stuffs the underwear into his trouser pocket.

> PHIL
> Oh, hi Lucy… I was expecting Angie..
>
> LUCY (*with a disapproving look over her glasses*)
> Obviously…..my sister not here then…?
>
> PHIL
> No I went out after lunch and haven't been back long. I thought you were her, she didn't say she was going anywhere.

LUCY goes out to ANGELA'S room and opens the door. PHIL follows. The bed is unmade. The drawers and wardrobe are open and ANGELA'S clothes are gone.

> PHIL (*surprised*)
> It looks like she's gone – where the hell could she have gone to..?
>
> LUCY
> Berlin, probably…

PHIL
Berlin? Why? She said we were going …What the
bloody hell is she up to!

LUCY
Old boyfriend at a guess… I did warn you about her.

*PHIL stands looking crestfallen. LUCY doesn't appear in the least
surprised at the course of events. She leaves the bedroom leaving
PHIL still standing there, staring.*

LUCY
Right, I'm off for a soak. Do the washing up will
you…?

Scene 43: EXT – PHILS CAR - DAY

Phil is sitting in his car in a gloomy rainy street in suburban England. Every now and then he raises his binoculars to his eyes and scribbles something in his notebook. He pours some tea from his flask and is about to take a sip when his mobile phone rings.

PHIL
Hello

LUCY
Phil, is that you?

PHIL
Yes, who's that?

LUCY
It's Lucy - Lucy Gordon from Switzerland – do you remember?

PHIL (*sighs to himself and says sarcastically*)
How could I forget…?

LUCY
Sorry..? It's a bad line

PHIL
Erm yeah … Hi Lucy! Course I remember. Did you - er - ever track Angie down again?

LUCY
Yes, she came back. I knew she would, of course. As soon as she had a problem. Turns out her old boyfriend in Berlin was married and didn't want to see her.

ANGIE (*snivelling in background, just audible over the phone*)
It was all that wife of his….

LUCY
So, as you can hear, she's back here safe and
sound

ANGELA *snivelling*
She was really horrid to me…tell Phil to come back. I
want him here….NOW!

LUCY
Ignore her Phil, she's having a little selfish five
minutes.

PHIL
Yes, I think I'd keep her at arms length if I were you.
I know what she's like now.

LUCY
The reason I'm ringing – I'm coming over to England
next week and I want to do a bit of checking up on
things. Would you be able to give me a hand..?

*Over the phone PHIL can hear ANGELA ranting in the in
background*

ANGELA
You bitch! You want him for yourself just like always.
You can't find your own blokes so you have to steal
mine! Don't you dare go to England!

LUCY (*cupping her hand over the phone*)
Look, Phil. I'm flying in on Monday afternoon . I'll call
you then, OK.

*PHIL hears the phone click as LUCY puts it down at her end.
He sighs to himself and returns to his surveillance work.*

Scene 44: EXT – OUSIDE BUNGALOW - DAY

PHIL's car is parked outside. He and LUCY are in the car, checking the address on a slip of paper.

> LUCY
> You're sure this is the place – it looks all shut up.

> PHIL
> Well, if the guy has retired he might have gone to live by the sea or something … but it's the only shot we've got. Let's give it a try.. eh?

> LUCY
> Well, OK but what are we going to say- we can't just come out with it – and anyway he's under no obligation to tell us anything anyway..

> PHIL
> We'll think of something

PHIL opens his door and goes to get out. LUCY hesitates.

> PHIL
> You coming then..?

> LUCY (takes deep breath)
> Yes – lets do it..

The two of them walk up the front path to the house and ring the door bell. The house looks quiet and empty. All the front curtains are tightly closed.

> PHIL
> Thought so – he's buggered off

> LUCY
> Do you mind!… we'll it looks as if you're right.

PHIL goes to look down the side of the house.

LUCY is about to walk back to the car when she notices one of the front curtains lift slowly and then drop quickly. The two of them walk up the front path to the house and ring the door bell. The house looks quiet and empty. All the front curtains are tightly closed.

>LUCY
>Phil! There's someone there, I've just seen a curtain move.....Phil!

PHIL's head pokes back round the side of the house.

>PHIL
>Come on, let's try the back

>LUCY
>But there's someone in there....

>PHIL
>All the better – they can let us in

PHIL disappears round towards the back of the house. LUCY sighs and then follows him reluctantly.

In contrast to the front, the back garden looks more lived in with washing on the line and rubbish by the dustbin.

PHIL starts peering through the windows but the back door is quickly pulled half open and a timid face looks out. The man is balding, has glasses and a thin, greying beard. He is wearing a still collared shirt and blue cardigan and seems to be shaking like a leaf.

>WARNETT
>Who are you---- what are you doing here??

>PHIL
>Mr Warnett,? We wondered if we could talk to you..?

WARNETT (*mumbling nervously*)
Talk to me? You can't **talk** to me.!.. You haven't
made an appointment....no...no, it's not possible. I
don't **talk** to people

*WARNETT goes to shut the door but LUCY steps in and puts her
hand over his, trying the softer approach*

LUCY
Please Mr Warnett... just for a few minutes? You did
some work for my mother – Margaret Gordon – do
you remember....?

WARNETT (still being evasive)
No, I don't see people without an appointment, , no, I
couldn't... Talk to me? Gordon?? – Margaret
Gordon? Your mother...?..

*WARNETT succeeds in shutting the door. LUCY moves her fingers
just in time. She and PHIL look at each.*

PHIL
Well, what do you think that was all about...?

LUCY
I don't know but he's obviously worried about
something. Let me try again.

*LUCY tries the door. It opens and she cautiously goes into the
kitchen, motioning PHIL to stay outside.*

Scene 45: INT – INSIDE HOUSE- DAY

LUCY creeps through the house to find WARNETT sitting in the living room in the dark with his head in his hands, muttering to himself…

>WARNETT (*to himself…*)
>They said that was it…. no more they said… I could go they said…

>LUCY
>Mr Warnett… ?

WARNETT looks up startled

>WARNETT
>You're still here…? I said you had to go!

>LUCY (*trying to calm him*)
>Yes I will go, I promise… But you are the only one who can help me find out about my mother, Mr Warnett… You did know my mother didn't you?

>WARNETT
>Margaret Gordon – yes! but they said that was it, it would all be over…
>She didn't have an appointment either – they just came in….

>LUCY
>Yes she was very demanding wasn't she..

>WARNETT
>And she was **your** mother…?I thought she was An.. An.. what was he name – Baz's erm.. Norman Davison's thingy…

>LUCY
>Angela! Angela Davison – yes she's my sister.

WARNETT
Angela! Yes, that's it – pretty blonde girl – shame really. Baz made me do it…She's your **sister**…? , You mean Margaret Gordon had two daughters…? Oh no this is awful… Awful!

WARNETT jumps up and goes to the drawer. He takes some tablets and gulps down some water. LUCY motions towards the kitchen..

LUCY
Shall I make some tea…?

WARNETT makes a positive motion towards the kitchen and sits back down. LUCY goes into the kitchen and makes a pot of tea. PHIL has been frantically trying to hear what had been going on. LUCY motions him in but indicates that he should keep quiet. LUCY takes the tea into the living room and sits down opposite WARNETT.

WARNETT *(as if a different person – now sharp and active)*
I don't know how you found me and I don't want to know. I am retired now , you understand, through ill health

LUCY
Yes, I was very sorry to hear that you…

WARNETT
What I am about to tell you is between the two of us only. If it ever comes out, I shall deny all knowledge of it – understood?

WARNETT makes a cautious glance towards the window as if he feels he is being watched. He edges forward and LUCY does the same.

WARNETT *(in a low voice)*
I was working for Rempel Smith & Dennis- the law firm that took over your mother – Mrs Gordon's - affairs.

She was living is Spain, you know – oh yes of course you do – and they, well, she needed a UK agent to handle her share dealings.

One day, I was working on some papers for another client and they all turned up.

LUCY
All….?

WARNETT
Yes, all of them…

We, see the scene in flashback with WARNETT's voice as narrator.

WARNETT is in his office looking at some papers. The door opens and people come in unannounced. Warnett looks up annoyed. Baz comes in and appears to take over.

WARNETT (*voice over*)
Baz Davison, he was the senior partner – my boss if you like, Norman his brother – never really like him , Mrs Gordon, Angela and the company doctor.. Well, I thought they were supposed to have been in Spain….

The people in the flashback shake hands and sit down

WARNETT (*voice over*)
Anyway, Baz introduced me to them and then Norman took his wife… er Angela.. that's your sister.. out of the room.

He then told me that Mrs Gordon had asked to be put into a home as Angela couldn't look after her anymore.

I looked at Mrs Gordon, she looked straight ahead and didn't say a word.

Baz said she'd been certified incapable of looking after herself by two doctors in Spain and showed me a piece of paper written in Spanish.

Baz said that I had to give her daughter Power of Attorney to act for her and sign things and I said I'd have to interview her and satisfy myself that she was incapable.

Baz said that he's already done that but, as he was related to the beneficiary of the order he couldn't sign it himself. He'd already drawn it up and just wanted me to sign it…

I tried to tell him that it was most irregular but he insisted… He threatened that he would stop my early retirement and that I'd have to carry on working despite my nervous problem.

The scene returns briefly to the living room.

>LUCY
>Yes, it must have terrible for you… what happened then?

>WARNETT
>Well, I objected to being ordered to just sign something I didn't agree with. I turned to Mrs Gordon – your mother – and asked her if she knew the importance of the document that she had signed.

Return to flashback:

>WARNETT (*Voice over*)
>She looked at me and coldly stated that she had not signed it and was having nothing to do with any such nonsense.…

>I looked at Baz who motioned to me that she was obviously crazy.. and then I tried a different approach.

So, Angela's going to look after things for you..? I asked her... she replied that she was a dimwitted girl who couldn't even look after herself properly and that Norman was manipulating her to do evil things. She said that she wanted to live with her other daughter.

At that point Baz ushered her out of the room and left me with the company doctor.

Then Baz came back in and the doctor said that Mrs Gordon was obviously delusioned to think that she had two daughters. The doctor said that he concurred with the Spanish diagnosis and he signed the Order of Attorney.

The DOCTOR signs the paper and we see BAZ try to get WARNETT to sign. An argument ensues.

WARNETT (*Voice over*)
I couldn't sign because there wasn't enough evidence. It was all too quick for my liking. I hadn't been told....

Back to the living room.

LUCY
But you did sign, didn't you...?

WARNETT
I had to – he made me.

In flashback:

WARNETT (*Voice over*)
Baz said that the doctor would block my early retirement. I'd have to stay until I was 65 ... another 18 years of those bastards and their dodgy deals ...I couldn't .. I really couldn't..... I'm so sorry...

Scene fades back to living room. WARNETT is now losing his previous composure and going back to being a shivering wreck. He begins to sob into the cushion. LUCY puts her hand on Warnett's shoulder to comfort him

> LUCY
> Yes, Mr Warnett, I'm sure it must have been terrible for , you. Er... Where could I get a copy of the Attorney deed? That could be very important.. do you know..?
>
> WARNETT (still sobbing)
> Not possible – they are destroyed as soon as the person dies - oh it was so awful… terrible

LUCY quietly gets up to go, motions to PHIL and they both leave.

Scene 46: EXT- FRONT GARDEN – DAY

PHIL and LUCY walk away from the house in silence. They get into the car.

> LUCY
> I feel sorry for him actually

> PHIL
> Yes but if he signed a paper that he shouldn't then he could be done for it…

> LUCY
> Oh, come on. You can't prosecute someone in his condition. You saw the state of him

> PHIL
> So, what do you want to do now?

> LUCY
> Well, from what Mr Warnett said, it sounds as if poor Angie didn't really have a clue what was going on.
>
> It was Baz and Norm plotting all along. I think it's time to confront Mr so-called-Big Baz Davison.

> PHIL (*starting the car's engine*)
> Right! Where to, boss?

> LUCY
> I'll go and see Mr Davison. I should be safe enough in a solicitors' office in Haworth. I'd like you to go and see what Norman is up to – where he's living, where the kids are - what his financial situation is OK?

> PHIL
> You're sure you'll be alright? I mean if we're right and there has been a cover up, then Baz Davison isn't going to be took keen for you to be talking to people about it.

                    LUCY
                    Don't worry about me.

She opens the car door and steps out

                    I'll get a taxi - see you back at the hotel later, OK

*PHIL motions a wave at her and pulls the passenger door shut. He
takes his A to Z from the glove compartment and looks for Norman's
street. He drives off down the road tooting his horn at LUCY as he
drives past her. She is walking down towards the main road.*

Scene 47: EXT – SOLICITOR'S OFFICE – DAY

We see LUCY getting out of a taxi in a busy picturesque shopping street in a small Yorkshire town. She goes into a smart looking building It is an old fashioned looking place but with a very expensive looking sign by the door reading "Rempel, Smith and Dennis – Solicitors"

LUCY goes to the reception desk.

> LUCY
> I'd like to see Mr Davison please – Barry Davison
>
> RECEPTIONIST (*coldly*)
> Do you have an appointment?
>
> LUCY
> No I don't but he'll see me, I'm sure
>
> RECEPTIONIST (*more coldly*)
> He doesn't see anyone without an appointment
>
> LUCY (*leaning forward and looking over her glasses*)
> That may be so but I'm sure he'll **see me**!
>
> RECEPTIONIST (*now looking decidedly frosty*)
> Who shall I say asking for him?
>
> LUCY
> Miss Gordon – Lucy Gordon.
>
> RECEPTIONIST (*picking up her telephone*)
> One moment please... hello there's a Miss Gordon to see Baz...no er Lucy

She turns back to Lucy

> It was Lucy Gordon , you said

LUCY
Yes, I'm Angela's sister – or should that be
<u>Margaret's other daughter..?</u>

Before she has time to finish the sentence a door swings open and a hot and bothered looking Baz walks in trying to smile. He approaches Lucy and holds his hand out as if to shake hers but then doesn't.

BAZ
Lucy! What a pleasant surprise. You should have told me , you were coming. I've got appointments all afternoon. How's er Angie..?

LUCY
Angie's fine – safely away from that drunkard brother of yours at long last.

BAZ's smile fades completely. He casts a glance over to the receptionist and motions LUCY to follow him. They go into a side waiting room with a couple of chairs and a table. They both sit down. BAZ makes an attempt to put his smile back on again.

BAZ
So what brings you to this neck of the woods, then? Bit of a long way from Sweden, after all!

LUCY
I work in Switzerland actually not Sweden but I'd actually much rather talk about Spain really.

BAZ
Ah Spain! Ok - damned hot – rowdy tourists - cheap beer – not much more to say really. Ask me another!

LUCY
How about the property market in Spain?

Erm ooh – property -? Not really my department, old
girl. If you want to buy somewhere abroad, you
ought to talk to old Squiffy Woofs in our
conveyancing department. He's just got himself a
little place in the Algarve – yes Squiffy's the man.

*BAZ goes to stand up, in the hope that the conversation is at an end
but LUCY grabs his jacket sleeve and sits him down again., pushing
her face close up into his.*

LUCY
I don't want to **buy** somewhere – I believe I'm
supposed to have **inherited** somewhere – ring any
bells?

*BAZ's expression changes completely and he begins to look a little
worried*

BAZ
Oh – you know about that do you?

LUCY (*bluffing*)
Yes, Angela has told me all about it – what you did to
Mother …

BAZ
Now come on Lucy, that's not fair – your mother was
very old…

LUCY
Yes, and she'd have lived to be a lot older if it hadn't
have been for you lot plotting and scheming!

She calms down a bit

And then there's the question of the house….

BAZ
Oh, , you know about that as well….well, it was your mother 's money to do with as she wished…

LUCY
And why exactly would mummy want to suddenly buy a bloody great house in Spain? She hated the sun, hated the heat. She didn't even like going to Wales - let alone abroad!

BAZ (*as if quoting from a brochure*)
Presumably she wanted to spend a quite peaceful retirement in the bosom of her loving family.

LUCY
Crap! She hated Norman, hated kids and hated people scrounging off her – the last thing she would have wanted would have been to go of and live with them all in Spain.

BAZ
Well, as I said, it was her money to do with as she wanted…..

Scene 48: *EXT – RESIDENTIAL STREET – DAY*

PHIL has arrived outside Norman's house. It is the same one from which he had helped ANGELA escape some months before. The house now looks very tatty and the garden is all overgrown. One of the upstairs windows is broken and someone had spray painted "PERV" across the front door.

PHIL takes his trusty clipboard and knocks at the house next door. An old lady answers.

> PHIL
> Sorry to bother you madam. Do you know if Mr Davison still lives next door?

> OLD LADY (*looking at him with suspicion*)
> Are you another reporter? If so, clear off I've nothing to say!

She goes to close the door. PHIL tries to stop her but doesn't succeed. The door slams and PHIL goes round the corner to get a view of the back of the house.

The back garden gate is swinging off it's hinges and the dustbin is piled up with black rubbish bags that are also strewn across the back yard. The kitchen door appears to be open a crack. PHIL carefully negotiates the garden detritus and looks round the side of the door. On the floor near the step is a brown window envelope – like a gas bill – PHIL picks it up and looks at the name of the address. It is addressed to Mr N Davison. PHIL pushes the door open a little wider. There is no sign of life. He enters the house.

The kitchen is as messy as the garden with plates piled up in the sink and mouldy food wrappers all over the place. PHIL is about to go further into the house when he hears a noise somewhere close. He looks behind him to see NORMAN coming up from the cellar carrying a coal shovel full of coal. On seeing PHIL, NORMAN tips the coal onto the floor and brandishes the shovel in a menacing fashion

> NORMAN
> Who the hell are you? What do you want?

PHIL
Erm – Mr – er Davison?

NORMAN
Yes! What do you want? Leave me alone! I haven't done anything ok – the police have said so - just piss off and leave me alone..

PHIL holds his hands out in front of him to try and reassure NORMAN. He also tries to edge towards the door and make an escape. As he does so, NORMAN gets there first and slams the door shut.

NORMAN
Come on, who are you? – press, vigilante? Cuz if you are I'll give you a good hiding right now.

NORMAN goes to raise the shovel. PHIL covers his head with his hands and calls out in desperation

PHIL
No! Norman please! – I'm a friend – really - I've got a message from Angela!

At the mention of Angela, Norman is taken aback and lowers the shovel.

NORMAN
Angela – what my Angie? What do you know about her- where is   she?

PHIL
Can we go and sit down – somewhere more comfortable?

NORMAN motions with the spade towards the dining room. They walk through and sit in the lounge, which is also awash with newspapers, letters, final demands and other litter.

Scene 49: INT – SOLICITORS OFFICE – DAY

*We switch back to BAZ's waiting room. LUCY and BAZ are arguing.
Baz is trying to leave. LUCY is becoming more an more angry.*

> BAZ (*opening the door*)
> Lucy! You just can't go around making unfounded
> allegations with no proof. I could sue you for slander
> right here and now…!
>
> LUCY
> I have documentary evidence that you were involved
> and I will have no qualms whatsoever about
> reporting you!

*LUCY storms out of the room and out of the building. BAZ quickly
darts into a side office and speaks to a junior clerk. The clerk picks
up his coat and sidles out of the building. We look up the street and
see him following LUCY towards town.*

Scene 50: INT – NORMAN'S LIVING ROOM – EVE

PHIL and NORMAN are still talking in the living room. NORMAN has got through a whole bottle of whisky. Phil is looking for an opportunity to leave.

> NORMAN
> Course, the worst thing – the worst thing ol' mate – d'you know what's the worst thing?

> PHIL
> What's the worst thing, Norman?

> NORMAN
> After all I did for her – and then – after she left me – with that piece of dirt

NORMAN grabs PHIL by the collar and shouts into his face

> NORMAN
> Then……then…. She only goes and rings the bloody local paper and tells'em I'm a pervert! Could you believe that? Me! Her own husband and she calls me a pervert!

> PHIL
> So why'd she do that, mate?

> NORMAN
> Cuz she's a spiteful cow, I dunno – you tell me. I'm not anyway. The police came an checked it out they said I was OK. Not that people round here take any notice of that of course…

> PHIL *(goes to get up)*
> Listen mate, I've got to go.

> NORMAN
> No – don't go, we were just getting on cosy then.

PHIL (*stands up and makes for the door*)
No, I must go – got work to do.

NORMAN (*struggles to get up*)
You said you had a message from Angie – what was
it?

*PHIL looks dumbfounded for a moment then remembers something
he ahs in his wallet. He fishes it out of his pocket. He takes out a
photo of ANGELA. It bears a message saying "Sorry, Angie XX".
He gives the photo to NORMAN*

PHIL
She wanted you to have this.

*NORMAN grasps the photo in both hands and stares at it. PHIL
takes the opportunity to slip out of the house. NORMAN looks up and
calls after him*

NORMAN
Oi - where did you get this? Who the hell are you
anyway?

*NORMAN rushes to the front door and looks down the road but can
only see PHIL's car tail lights disappearing into the distance.*

Scene 51: EXT - HOTEL ENTRANCE – NIGHT

PHIL'S car pulls up in the hotel car park and he gets out. He goes into the main entrance of the hotel. As he passes, we see that the solicitor's clerk is hunched down in a car parked in the shadows, obviously watching the hotel. The clerk makes a call on his mobile phone and the camera follows PHIL into the hotel reception.
PHIL picks up his key from reception and then sees LUCY sitting in the bar waving to him. He goes over and sits on the stool next to her.

>   LUCY
> How did it go then? Did you find Norman?

>   PHIL
> Fine... well, fine if you count being almost being brained with a coal shovel as good progress...

>   LUCY
> Ooh dear – but, you're all right though..?

>   PHIL
> Yes, I managed to talk my way out of it. But Nasty Norman's in a mess.

>   LUCY
> Come on let's go and eat. You can tell me all about it over dinner. It's all left me rather peckish.

LUCY stands up and puts her coat on ready to go. PHIL looks longingly at the bar and reluctantly follows her

>   LUCY
> The menu here doesn't look too good so I thought we'd try that place up the road, OK? We can walk then and you can have a drink if you want..

>   PHIL
> Yes, I could do with a drink..

As PHIL and LUCY leave the hotel, we see the CLERK furtively slip out of his car and go in the main entrance.

Scene 52: INT – RESTAURANT – NIGHT

LUCY and PHIL are at table in the corner of the restaurant. They have finished eating and are drinking after dinner coffee. The fact that most of the other tables have been cleared shows that it is now quite late in the evening.

                    LUCY
          But the kids are OK, though?

                    PHIL
          Far as I could tell .. . It was difficult without asking a
          direct question. He was already suspicious as hell –
          not surprising I don't s'pose – not in   the
          circumstances…

PHIL sips his coffee before continuing

                    PHIL
          Sonya – the snobbish daughter – he called her -
          she's off at university doing well, apparently. And the
          boy has moved in with one of his mates. Didn't like
          having to hand over his dole money for food and
          help with the housework, according to Norman. Then
          again, looking at the state of the place, I wouldn't
          fancy living there either to be honest!

                    LUCY
          So he's certainly not living a life of luxury off any ill
          gotten gains - that's for sure.

                    PHIL
          Exactly – but enough about him - come on – you've
          got to tell me - how did it go with Big Bad Baz?

                    LUCY (*looking sheepish*)
          To be honest, I think I might have mucked it up a bit.

                    PHIL
          How come?

LUCY
Well, I thought I'd play it all aloof and cool and
efficient and try and pick his brains but, in the end, I
lost my temper and started accusing him of all sorts
of things.

PHIL
Hmm – not the best thing to do with the senior
partner in a firm of solicitors…

LUCY
Well, it is my mum we're talking about. I just got a
bit emotional.
Anyway, after I'd left there I went and saw a chap
that a contact at the bank had recommended. He
was quite helpful but it all gets more complicated by
the minute.

PHIL
So, what did you find out?

*LUCY launches into an account of her meeting with the bank. We
see the conversation in flashback.*

*She is sitting in a plush office with a banking type in a blue pinstripe
suit.*

LUCY
So, based on that very sketchy information, what are
your thoughts?

*The BANKER sits back in his chair and thinks for a moment before
answering. He then draws himself forward and replies.*

BANKER
Well, if you want my honest opinion , you're on a
very   sticky   wicket.   With   no   documentation
whatsoever, there's no case to prove.

LUCY is about to say something but the BANKER continues

However, off the record I can tell you what I think
could have happened. This is just between me and ,
you of course – if anyone else gets to hear about it,
we never had this conversation – OK?

LUCY
Why do people keep saying that, I wonder? ....yes
OK!

BANKER
Right, you remember the big property boom in the
early 1980s when there was also the big time share
thing?

LUCY nods, fully attentive

*The scene returns to the restaurant with PHIL and LUCY putting their
coats on.*

PHIL
So do you really think that's what happened?
Sounds a bit far fetched.

LUCY
Well, without proof we can't be sure.

They leave the restaurant and begin walk slowly down the street

LUCY
But there was that mysterious phone call I got from
that bloke in Spain that time – d'you remember me
telling you..?

PHIL
That's right – John or Jim or something..? So, you
think there's some truth in it then?

LUCY
Yes he said they'd bought some flats. That would
certainly explain why they needed a mortgage to buy

the house. Mummy's money would have been enough for that otherwise – from the sale of her house in England.

                    PHIL
          "Curiouser and curiouser said Alice.."

LUCY wraps her coat tighter around her and slides her arm through PHIL's. They carry on walking up the road and back to the hotel.

LUCY goes up to her room and, as she opens the door, we see that her room has been ransacked. She gasps and rushes down the hall to find PHIL. When she arrives at PHIL's room, we see PHIL looking over a similar scene.

                    LUCY
          My room's the same – who could have done it?

PHIL turns to LUCY and raises his eyebrows

                    PHIL
          Well, we've certainly ruffled someone's feathers!
          There's no-one here now - I've checked - You stay
          while I go and fetch the manager.

Scene 53: INT - HOTEL BREAKFAST ROOM – DAY

It is now morning and LUCY and PHIL are having breakfast in the hotel. LUCY is counting out on her fingers the things that she needs to replace following last night's raid

> LUCY.
> And there's my French perfume – bloody expensive that was. It spilled all over my other jacket . The jacket will probably come up ok but they don't make that perfume any more..
>
> You don't really believe it was an opportunist thief – like the manager said, do you..?
>
> PHIL
> Well, we're hardly the pick of the crop at this hotel are we? Have , you seen all those Mercs outside. That woman in the reception last night was wearing so much gold I thought she'd fall over...
>
> LUCY
> Yes   - and it was only our two rooms that were broken into....
>
> PHIL
> Exactly. There has to be a connection with our enquires yesterday. Now think very carefully . , You must have said something to someone to get them worried enough to commit burglary – Now think!

LUCY looks pensive for a moment then her face lights up.

> LUCY
> Of course – but no it couldn't be –
>
> PHIL
> What? Come on - spit it out

LUCY
When I was at Baz's office. I'd completely forgotten
about it – I'd got into a fearful temper as you know –
but I think I may have inadvertently said that we had
written proof that he'd been up to no good….

PHIL
Well that's it then – Big Bad Baz must have sent
someone to follow , you and then go through our
rooms and steal the evidence!

LUCY
But we haven't got any evidence!

PHIL (*draws himself closer and speaks in a low
voice*)
But they don't know that do they…

LUCY
Ooh – you mean…?

PHIL
Exactly! They must think you have some documents
hidden somewhere that incriminate them . Therefore
they must have done something that they want to
cover up. We are definitely on the right track - but
where to go now?

Scene 54: EXT - PHILS CAR – DAY

LUCY and PHIL are driving through the picturesque Yorkshire countryside.

> PHIL
> OK so there's nothing suspicious in with your mums bits of furniture. Hey – did you see that bloke's face light up when he thought we were coming to take it away..!

> LUCY
> Poor Mummy! To think that's all that's left of her memory. A couple of chairs and a table lamp.

> PHIL
> Yeah – I suppose Nasty Norm flogged off all the good stuff ages ago.

> LUCY (beginning to cry)
> I wish I'd known she was here – I'd have come and visited her. She could have come and lived with me... I didn't even know where she was...

PHIL puts his hand over on LUCY's arm to comfort her.

> PHIL
> Hey, come on – you did everything you could. If they moved and didn't tell, you where they were , you couldn't have been expected to do any more...

> LUCY
> Yes, I suppose so but, thinking of her in that old folks home – she didn't even like Yorkshire...!

> PHIL
> Hey – maybe that's it.

> LUCY (*cheering up a bit*)
> Maybe that's what?

PHIL
The old people's home. Maybe she left something there that Norm and Baz overlooked... surely it's worth a try..!

LUCY
Well, you never know. It's not far from here. Let's give it a go. , You'll have to turn round.

The car comes to a grinding halt, PHIL reverses down a farm track and the cur turns back the way it was coming. We see it driving off into the distance.

Scene 55: EXT – RESIDENTIAL HOME – DAY

We see PHIL's car parked outside The Byron Dobson Home For Retired Folk. It still looks a very remote and forbidding place. Switch to inside view. PHIL and LUCY are talking to the MANAGER in his office.

> MANAGER
> So, can you actually prove that you are Mrs Gordon's daughter..? We were led to believe that she only had the one , you see...
>
> LUCY (*fumbling in the inside pocket of her raincoat*)
> Yes, of course, I've got my er...

LUCY takes out a handful of documents and sorts through them. PHIL sighs and looks out of the window in an animated fashion.

> PHIL (*aside*)
> He's not going to help, I could tell it the moment we walked in..
>
> LUCY (*ignoring Phil*)
> There, my birth certificate and my passport – how's that?

The manager takes the documents and looks at them in a very unconvinced way...

> MANAGER
> Yes, thank you

The MANAGER returns the documents to LUCY

> MANAGER
> Well, I'm afraid you had a rather wasted journey. We don't have anything that belonged to your mother. The family – erm that's your family, of course – took all her effects after the funeral – we needed the room you see.

PHIL goes to stand up.

PHIL
Well, we'd better head off then..

LUCY
Nothing in the safe, then? Nothing she might have given you and you forgot about?

MANAGER
Nothing I can assure you.

PHIL
Any way, we ought to…

LUCY
You are sure…?

MANAGER
Quite sure

PHIL
Right! so…

LUCY
What about her room? Could we see her room?

MANAGER
Well, it does have another occupant now…

LUCY
Oh please, it would mean so much to me to see her room – just for a moment..?

MANAGER (*in submission*)
Oh, very well. But just for a moment - and only so long as you don't disturb Mrs Smethurst.

The three of them stand up and the MANAGER leads the way out of his office and up the stairs in the hall. They then go along the landing

*leading to the room that used to be Margaret's. The MANAGER taps
lightly on the door and opens it a crack.*

> MANAGER
> Mrs Smethhurst – are you at home..?

MANAGER turns to PHIL and LUCY

> MANAGER
> She's not there – so you have a quick peek.

*The MANAGER opens to door wider so that LUCY and PHIL can see
inside it but he stands in the doorway to make sure that they cannot
enter.*

> LUCY (*starting to cry gently*)
> This is where she spent her last lonely days – all on
> her own – poor mummy…

> MANAGER
> Well, she wasn't lonely that's for sure. She was the
> lire and soul of the place – when she was in the right
> mood!

> LUCY (*sniffing back the tears*)
> Yes, I can imagine she was… Tell me are any of her
> friends still here..?

> MANAGER
> Er – friends ? Yes I think…. er.

*MANAGER turns and walks along the hall a little way and looks in at
one of the open doors*

> MANAGER
> Mrs Rimes – good day to you….there are some
> people here – related to Mrs Gordon – you
> remember Mrs Gordon don't , you…

HILDA's VOICE (*from inside room*)
Margaret! Of course – ooh its not that nasty one is
it..?

MANAGER
No, Mrs Rimes, Lord Lucan's dead – remember..?

*HILDA's head peeps cautiously round the door. She sees that it is
isn't Lord Lucan and her manner lightens.*

HILDA
Oh, do come on in.

*As LUCY walks past the MANAGER he grabs her by the arm and
whispers in her ear*

MANAGER
Just ought to warn you - She loves company but is
as mad as a hatter. Forgets everything and
everyone in a flash … so don't take too much notice
of what she says

HILDA ushers LUCY and PHIL into her room

HILDA
So, you want to talk about Margaret? Would you like
some tea?

HILDA starts fussing over making tea.

LUCY
Did you know my mother well Mrs er, Rimes..?

HILDA (*with her hack to the rest of the room*)
Your mother? Never met the woman..!

LUCY and PHIL swap a laboured glance.

LUCY
But the Manager just said that , you were a great
friend of hers – Margaret Gordon

HILDA (*turning with kettle in hand*)
Oh Margaret yes – lovely woman – wicked sense of humour...

LUCY
Yes, well she was my mother...

HILDA
Your mother...? So , you're....

LUCY
Lucy that's right! I was living in Switzerland – I never even knew she was here.

HILDA (*bringing tea pot and cups over to small table by the window*)
Margaret's other daughter! Well I never! Course she talked about you a lot...

LUCY (*taking cup from HILDA*)
Did she?

HILDA (*giving cup to PHIL*)
But everyone else thought she was imagining it.

LUCY
Did they?

HILDA (*leaning closer to LUCY*)
Some of the people in here are a bit funny , you see...

LUCY (*nodding solemnly*)
Oh, I see..

HILDA
But I'd seen a photo – she kept it hidden in her purse, you know...

LUCY (*brightening up*)
Did she….really?

HILDA
Yes – wearing a pretty frock – green and white it was…

LUCY
Yes – I remember that - I wore it for my cousin's wedding – I must have been about fifteen

HILDA
But they took all her stuff, you know. Her daughter what was her name..? Audrey or …

LUCY
Angie..?

HILDA
Yes, that's it Angie – and her horrid husband

PHIL (*chipping in*)
That's Norman

HILDA
Very rude young lad he was…

LUCY
So she didn't leave anything behind…

HILDA
No luvvy, it all went…although….

LUCY
Yes?

HILDA
There was one day she came in and asked me to hide something… she was expected Andie and ….

LUCY
Angie and Norman..?

HILDA
Yes. That's right. And she wanted to keep those
things out of their way...

PHIL and LUCY swap glances

PHIL
That could be what all the fuss is about, y'know..

*HILDA gets up from the table and starts looking through her chest of
drawers*

HILDA
Envelope it was – yellow one – where did I put it?

LUCY
It doesn't matter if you can't find it now – we can
always come back another day

PHIL (*throws a furious glance*)
But of course, if you can find it NOW, that would be
GREAT – wouldn't it Lucy..?

LUCY
Well, yes it would really, I suppose

*HILDA continues to fish through her drawers and eventually stands
up triumphantly clutching an A4 sized buff envelope.*

HILDA
Found it! – I knew it was here somewhere. I kept it
hidden in case that Nigel came in here too

PHIL
Norman, you mean….yes, very wise…

HILDA
I'm sure she wanted you to have it. Well, she
certainly didn't want Andie to get her hands on it did
she... she was most insistent...Margaret was.. One
day my other daughter will come and take me away
from here she used to say....

LUCY
God, I wish I knew she was here.... I could have
come..

HILDA
Don't you worry, dear she was all right. Better here
than living with those parasites...

Scene 56: INT – FLAT HALLWAY – DAY

ANGELA is in a bit of a panic. KARL is not there and she's not sure what to do next. She searches frantically in her bag and pulls a piece of a paper out of her purse. She picks up the telephone and dials the number from the scrap of paper.

The scene switches and we see a telephone ring in a brightly coloured and airy room. A voice in the back ground calls "Senor – telefono!!"

We see a pair of feet emerging from a swimming pool outside, walk across the sun drenched patio, through French doors into the room and a mans's hand picks up the phone.

We switch back to ANGELA in the flat:

> ANGELA
> Thank god I've found , you… what are you doing there – you didn't tell me you were going?

Switch back to sunny villa. The man is standing in the shadows so that we can't see who it is – just to add a bit of mystery.

> MAN IN SHADOWS
> What do you expect? You've gone and shacked up with your old boyfriend again..

> ANGELA
> Yes, but….

> MAN IN SHADOWS
> You think I'm going to chase all over Europe trying to track you down to ask your permission to go and stay in my own house??

> ANGELA
> **My** house – if you don't mind… Any way- who are there with…?

MAN IN SHADOWS
Well, you know I'd much rather shag you - of course
- but if you do insist on running off, there's always
the odd servant or two here to keep me going.

ANGELA
How dare you …. Listen I need your help.. It's Lucy.
She says she's found some documents. She says
she knows what we did! Can that be true?

*Switch back to MAN in SHADOWS – the camera moves slowly
round and we see that it is BAZ.*

BAZ
Well, she's been sticking her hooter in all over the
places – with the damned bloody detective friend of
hers. It wouldn't surprise me. Why the hell do you
think I'm shacked up here. I was due some holiday
any way – thought it might be a good time – till the
heat wears off.

ANGELA
Heat wears off…! The heat's on me – you selfish
arsehole,   not you!   I signed the cheque –
remember?

BAZ
Exactly – and I was just following your instructions
as your legal representative – at least that's what all
the papers say…..

ANGELA (*sounding more desperate*)
So what am I going to do now..?

BAZ
Well, , you could pay your sister back the 100.000
quid inheritance that , you diddled her out of…or…

ANGELA
Or…?

                    BAZ
          Get yourself a good lawyer, gal. Not me though, I'm
          on holiday.

*BAZ puts the phone down and slopes in the arms of a slim dark
haired girl in a bikini. ANGELA stands holding the phone to her ear,
speechless. After a minute of so of thought she begins to shake
uncontrollably   with   rage   and   slams   the   phone   down.*

                    ANGELA
          Bastard!

*ANGELA grabs her bag and raincoat and storms out of the flat,
slamming the door behind her. It doesn't shut properly and swings
open again.*

Scene 57: EXT – BLOCK OF FLATS – DAY

WE see ANGELA storm out of the main entrance of the block of flats in floods of tears. She marches off down the street, knocking into passers- by as she goes. On the other side of the busy street A taxi pulls up. LUCY and PHIL are in it having an animated discussion about who has money to pay the fare.

                    PHIL
          You're the international banking whizz kid so why is
          it down to me to have brought some German
          money?

                    LUCY
          God Phil, we're in Berlin. What do you think they
          spend here?

                    PHIL
          Firstly , you didn't tell me were coming to Berlin.
          Secondly, you didn't give me a chance to change
          any money at the airport cuz you were in such a
          rush to get here.

                    LUCY
          Well, I'm worried about Angie... She sounded funny
          on the phone.. .and please don't tell me there's
          nothing new in that – I know – but she is still my
          sister....

                    PHIL
          Yes - who just happens to have cheated you out of
          your inheritance – can't we get her to pay for the
          bloody taxi?

                    LUCY
          Ok wait here.

LUCY jumps out of the taxi, leans over to the driver to explain that she'll be right back. She crosses the road and goes into the apartment block. A couple of minutes later she comes back looking anxious. She opens the car door and gets back in.

LUCY
She's not there she's gone. The caretaker saw her
crush off a minute or so ago.

(*to taxi driver*) Bitte weiter fahren – hier entlang

Let's see if we can catch her up. I really want to give
her that letter. It'll make her feel better.

Scene 58: EXT – BRIDGE OVER RIVER - DAY

We are in a suburb of Berlin – this can be seen from tall buildings and appropriate monuments in the distance. In the foreground, Angela is standing on the middle of the bridge looking out down the river. There are a few passers-by but it is not busy.

After a few moments of silence, a taxi pulls up. LUCY gets out, waits a minute or so and then and comes over to ANGELA. PHIL is also there, he gets out of the taxi but hangs back to let the two sisters talk.

> LUCY
> Angie..? What's happening? What are you doing here all on your own?
>
> ANGELA *(still gazing into the distance, as if talking to herself)*
> This was where it all started....
>
> LUCY
> Sorry..?
>
> ANGELA
> It all began here...
>
> LUCY
> Come on, let's get you back to the hotel, we've got a lot of things to discuss...I've found some papers of mummy's...

ANGELA turns her head to look at her sister, tears now burning in her eyes

> ANGELA
> You know, don't you...
>
> LUCY
> Come on let's not stand out here, it's going to rain.

ANGELA
You <u>KNOW</u>! don't you ... about mummy and the
house and the money

*LUCY goes to touch ANGELA and reassure her but ANGELA pulls
away and gazes back out along the river again*

LUCY
Come on, none of that matters now - we can talk it
through, sort it all out, you know we can. Phil's got a
taxi, we'll all go back together and sort it all out.

ANGELA *(as if she has gone back into her dream)*
Berlin... 1968. You were her too – remember?

LUCY
Yes I was here then but what ...

ANGELA *(carries on as if she doesn't hear)*
A dashing young cavalry officer....I thought: he' ll do
.....he's got a good job for life

*Cut to black and white flashbacks of military dances, smart uniforms
pretty dresses as if ANGELA is remembering them, then back to the
present*

ANGELA *(as if quoting her mother..)*
It's a good life as an officer's wife – good pay , travel
the world, good pension . I told him I was pregnant.

LUCY
What, Norman...?

ANGELA
His family were rich. Big house – holiday home –
nice car. I thought "he'll do". I'll never have to work
again. I could be happy like mummy and daddy
were.

LUCY
Angie – what are you talking about? Come on , it's
cold standing here..

ANGELA (*now looking angry turns to look her
straight in the face*)
Can't you see? Don't you understand? I made it
happen! It was all me.

I tricked him into marrying me. Then I found out that
he gambled – had debts, no money, his family had
disinherited him... I was stuck - don't you see that -
trapped..! So the house – well, it seemed like my
only way out...

LUCY
So that's why you stole mummy's money – our
inheritance - my inheritance – to make up for it - .to
keep you in pretty dresses and make up and
shoes..? Oh Angie...

*ANGELA looks at her sister in horror with the belief that she has
really found out all that had gone on*

LUCY
But I've found this...

*LUCY takes a buff coloured envelope out of her coat to show
ANGELA*

I know what you did but it doesn't matter now –
really. I love you, , , you're still my sister. We can sort
it out .... please come home.

ANGELA - not really listening - becomes more irate

ANGELA
That idiot! That cretin! He screwed up!

ANGELA goes to grab the envelope

LUCY
Look Angie, I don't really know what you're talking
about but…

ANGELA
He said he'd got rid of it all. Said it would look like
Norman did it…! And now, you – like always - you
stuck your little piggy nose into my business. You've
ruined it all!

ANGELA lunges at LUCY. LUCY steps back to avoid the sharp
finger nails aimed at her face. ANGELA misses her footing and falls
forward. She trip across the chain rope barrier and falls over the
side of the bridge into the water.

LUCY watches the plunge in horror and turns to get help

LUCY
Phil ! Quick, help – she can't swim!

PHIL rushes over, the taxi driver close behind him. PHIL starts to
take his shoes and socks off while the taxi driver struggles to unhook
a life preserver from further along the bridge. LUCY is leaning over
the side straining to see where ANGELA has gone.

LUCY
I can't see her.. oh Phil, please do something!

PHIL dives in to the water and starts groping around to find ANGELA
in the depths. LUCY is screaming ANGELA's name from the bridge.
Passers by congregate to watch and help.

Scene 59: *EXT – BRIDGE OVER RIVER - NIGHT*

Several hours have passed since ANGELA fell into the water and it is now dark. The bridge has just bee reopened to traffic. There are police cars and ambulances standing around the scene with lights flashing. Police divers are packing their equipment away into one of the vehicles.

LUCY is sitting in the back of an ambulance with a blanket round her. Her face is all blotchy from crying and her mascara has run.   PHIL is also there, huddled in an aluminium blanket, having caught hypothermia in the water.

> LUCY
> She always hated me…I don't know why. She was always jealous - always wanted what *I* had but never shared any of **her** toys.. d'you know what I mean…?
>
> PHIL
> Sounds to me like she used everyone - not just you.
>
> LUCY
> But I feel so guilty! If only I'd
>
> PHIL
> If only you'd what…? Given in to her every time she tried it on… she'd have just been back for more and more.

PHIL leans across to reassure LUCY

> PHIL
> She _played_ the victim. That's what she was good at - twisted everything round to get her own way - told so many lies that after a while she didn't know what was true anymore.
>
> But in the end we were all victims – even that revolting Baz – he's had to take sick leave apparently. Yes, we were victims…. of her scheming.

Scene 60: EXT – GERMAN CEMETARY - DAY

A funeral is taking place. LUCY and PHIL are there as are KARL and BRADFORD, who seems more upset than anyone else. ANGELA's children are being comforted by a very sheepish looking BAZ who is keen to avoid eye contact with LUCY and PHIL.

The congregation begins to walk away from the grave side.

>LUCY
>You did the right thing, Karl. She always seemed to be happier in Germany. After all she came back to you in the end..

>KARL
>Yes, it's just a shame we didn't have more time... after all those years apart...

PHIL catches them up and they all get into Karl's car, which is parked outside the gate.

>KARL
>I hope you will please stay at the house for day or two..? We could talk about things. There's so much that I just don't understand....

>PHIL
>You and me both mate. I suppose now we'll never know what got into her...

>LUCY
>It's kind of you, Karl. We'll stay tonight but Phil and I have to go back to England tomorrow.

>PHIL
>Do we?

>LUCY
>Yes, tomorrow you're going to start earning the keep you've had off me for the past three weeks. *(digging him in the ribs)*

                PHIL
                Oh charming!

                LUCY
                No - seriously Karl, we're going to try and sort out
                the mess that Angela left the family affairs in. Lots of
                lawyers and accountants to see and files to read
                through...   Just the thing for a workshy private
                detective to get his teeth into...

                PHIL (*teasingly*)
                Work shy, huh! Now, you listen to me - wife to be....

The scene falls back into a Long Shot

*The cars all drive away slowly. The scene widens to view the
graveyard as a whole. A single solitary figure – a woman – dressed
in black with a heavy black veil – approaches from the shadows of
the church and stands by the graveside looking down into the hole.*

                PHIL (*voice over*)
                I tell you what – it's not going to be easy, getting
                everybody to co-operate with our enquires back
                home

                LUCY
                You're telling me... how will we ever be able to
                convince them she's really dead if they never found
                the body...

*The black clad lady throws something down into the grave and walks
away slowly. Camera moves in to look at grave and sees that
Angela's passport and jewellery have been dropped onto the top of
the coffin.*

The scene fades to end.

Closing theme
End credits roll.